WHAT REVIEWERS ARE SAYING ABOUT HELPING THE STRUGGLING ADOLESCENT . . .

This book has great potential to become *the* reference guide for parents, teachers, youth leaders, and Christian counselors who have contact with teenagers. Dr. Parrott has written a clear, well-documented, practical, and people-sensitive book that I can recommend warmly.

—*Gary R. Collins*
People Helpers International

Dr. Parrott has furnished a brilliant handbook for all who work with teens. It is required reading for my students in youth ministry.

—*Donald M. Joy*
Asbury Theological Seminary

Les Parrott has put his sensitive finger on the pulse of adolescent problems and has come up with an array of practical, effective helping techniques. His advice comes from his heart as well as from his extensive research.

—*Philip G. Zimbardo*
Stanford University

Les Parrott understands adolescents and what troubles them. He also understands parents and their concerns for their children. . . . Parents, teachers, and youth workers will make frequent use of the practical and biblically based handbook.

—*Stephen A. Hayner*
InterVarsity Christian Fellowship

Only on rare occasions does a book come across my desk that is intriguing, practical, and theoretically insightful. *Helping the Struggling Adolescent* is one of those rare books. Dr. Parrott's very readable style gives parents, youth ministers, and professionally trained therapists equal access to valuable psychological principles of adolescent development and personal ministry with young people.

—*G. Keith Olson*
Author of Counseling Teenagers

Dr. Parrott has assembled a compassion-based approach to helping young people in very practical and effective ways. I highly recommend *Helping the Struggling Adolescent* to pastors, counselors, youth workers, parents, educators, and any other adult seeking to guide young people into a hope-filled life.

—*Dub Ambrose*
Department of Youth
United Methodist Pub

Adolescence is an era of life that is, indeed, a
perspective, or overview, is immense. Dr. Parrott h
well.

—*Grace H. Ketterman, M.D.*
Author of Understanding Your Child's Problems

Helping the Struggling Adolescent is an excellent tool for counselors, youth workers, and parents. Dr. Parrott has an easy style that facilitates understanding the heart of the problem and how to assist each struggling child. This is a comprehensive book that I plan to use as a guide in raising my own child. If you have a child who is struggling with anything from suicide to sexual identity, this is a valuable resource for help.

—Stephen Arterburn
Founder, New Life Treatment Centers

Helping the Struggling Adolescent is a wonderful resource for anyone who counsels, ministers to, or *lives with* adolescents. The book is well-researched and documented. His warmth and poignant examples make this a supremely readable book.

—Robert S. McGee
Founder, Rapha Hospital Treatment Centers

Les Parrott speaks from a platform of professional understanding and practical experience. This book will provide very practical help to the counselor in the trenches. It is "user-friendly" with a solid base in the literature of counseling.

—Jay Kesler
President, Taylor University

Guiding teenagers through the adolescent years has become one of the most difficult tasks of our time. We need all the help we can get, and Les Parrott has provided a lot of it. Youth workers will find this book invaluable. Its practical advice built on sound research will meet a desperate need.

—Tony Campolo
Author of Growing Up in America

Unique and urgently needed is the best way to describe this practical book. Easy to read, it will be a welcomed resource by anyone ministering to adolescents, which includes parents as well.

—H. Norman Wright
Author of Crisis Counseling

Helping the
Struggling Adolescent:
A Counseling Guide

This book is intended to be used with a companion volume, *Helping the Struggling Adolescent: A Guide for Parents, Counselors, and Youth Workers*. The book may be ordered from the same source as this counseling guide under ISBN 0-310-57821-3.

Helping the Struggling Adolescent: A Counseling Guide

WITH 40 RAPID ASSESSMENT TESTS

Les Parrott III

ZondervanPublishingHouse
Academic and Professional Books
Grand Rapids, Michigan

A Division of HarperCollinsPublishers

Helping the Struggling Adolescent: A Counseling Guide
Copyright © 1993 by Les Parrott III

Requests for information should be addressed to:
Zondervan Publishing House
Academic and Professional Books
Grand Rapids, Michigan 49530

Edited by James E. Ruark
Cover design by Mark Veldheer

Library of Congress Cataloging-in-Publication Data

Parrott, Les.
    Helping the struggling adolescent : a counseling guide : with forty rapid assessment tests /
Leslie Parrott III.
        p.   cm.
    Companion volume to: Helping the struggling adolescent : a guide for parents, counselors, and
youth workers.
    ISBN 0-310-61511-9
    1. Teenagers—Psychological testing. 2. Teenagers—Counseling of. 3. Adolescent psycho-
therapy. I. Title.
BF724.25.P37   1993   93-8385
362.7'083—dc20   CIP

Printed in the United States of America

93 94 95 96 97 98 /   / 10 9 8 7 6 5 4 3 2 1

To a man who caught my vision
and gave me the tools for making it a reality,
Dr. Archibald D. Hart—my mentor and friend

CONTENTS

HOW TO USE THIS BOOK

Possessing a book sometimes becomes a substitute for reading it. That is not necessarily the case with this volume. *Helping the Struggling Adolescent: A Counseling Guide* is not meant to be read through like a novel. It is a reference tool to be used for improving the counseling work you do with adolescents.

This book is a companion volume to *Helping the Struggling Adolescent: A Guide to Thirty Common Problems for Parents, Counselors, and Youth Workers*. It is an extension of the first book and is designed to be used in conjunction with it.

This counseling guide is organized into two parts. Part One, consisting of three chapters, provides information specifically for the counselor of adolescents. Part II provides an introductory chapter on using and interpreting assessment tools. It also supplies copies of actual instruments that can be used in your work with young people.

Part II is the heart of this book, containing more than forty rapid-assessment instruments. Each of these paper-and-pencil tests is linked to a specific chapter—sometimes more than one—in the first volume. The instruments are presented in alphabetical order. However, the book contains a list of the instruments cross-indexed according to the problem area for ease in locating the ones you want. If you need an instrument for evaluating an adolescent's potential for an eating disorder, for example, you can look under "Eating Disorder" in the cross-referenced list (p. 39). There you will find six tests: (1) Are You Dying To Be Thin Scale, (2) Bulimia Test, (3) Concern Over Weight and Dieting Scale, (4) Eating Attitudes Test, (5) Goldfarb Fear of Fat Scale, and (6) Restraint Scale. Any or all of these instruments may be of use to you in working with the adolescent you are counseling.

"There are books of which the cover is the best part," said Charles Dickens. I hope you will find more than the cover of this volume to be useful. My prayer is that this book will help you enhance the efficiency and effectiveness of your counseling work with the young people in your care.

I am very grateful to several people who have played a crucial role in shaping this book. I am first of all indebted to the numerous authors, institutes, and companies who allowed me to reproduce their assessment instruments. I also want to acknowledge with thanks my colleagues at Seattle Pacific University and the University of Washington School of Medicine for permitting me the freedom to integrate my academic pursuits with clinical practice—and to be a writer.

A special word of thanks goes to Alan Basham, Don MacDonald, and

Michael Roe for their insightful suggestions and critiques. They helped me separate the wheat from the chaff. Sarah Timmons and Emily Spiger, my assistants, did an outstanding job of helping me organize this project and graciously took up the baton of permissions editors. Jim Ruark, my editor at Zondervan, managed this "struggling" project with wit, warmth, and generosity of spirit.

Finally, my affection and thanks to Leslie, who has once again shared her husband with a book project.

Part One

Special Issues in Counseling

1

Common Pitfalls
in Counseling Adolescents

A promising junior executive at IBM was involved in a risky venture for the company and managed to lose more than $10,000,000. The results were disastrous. When IBM's founder and president, Tom Watson, called the nervous executive into his office, the young man blurted, "I guess you want my resignation?" Watson said, "You can't be serious. We've just spent ten million dollars educating you!"

Fortunately, most mistakes are not as costly as the one this young executive made. And most companies can't absorb ten-million-dollar mistakes. But when it comes to counseling teenagers, every error has the potential for devastating results. We are not doomed to repeat counseling mistakes, however. We can learn to avoid the pitfalls others have encountered.

This chapter is designed to help you sidestep some of the most common counseling pitfalls. It is not meant to serve as an exhaustive listing of blunders made by counselors. Nor is it a catalog of the worst possible therapeutic errors. Rather, this list is representative of some of the most common mistakes made when counseling adolescents.

PREMATURE PROBLEM SOLVING

Frieda Fromm-Reichmann said, "The patient needs an experience, not an explanation." She could have said the same thing about struggling adolescents.

Trying to solve a young person's problem before the problem is fully understood is a common therapeutic mistake.[1] It takes patience and time to unwrap the salient features of a teenager's problem. Like a complex jigsaw puzzle with hundreds of interlocking pieces, a young person's struggle cannot be solved in a matter of minutes.

Consider Tracy, a high school senior with a 3.8 GPA, who says, "I'm really depressed, and I think it's because I bombed my English mid-term." As her counselor, you check out her symptoms and quickly recognize that her self-

15

assessment seems accurate. Tracy expects to receive high marks, and failing an important exam is traumatic for her. You wonder whether the expectations she holds for her academic performance are unrealistic. You gently search, asking questions that may or may not enforce your hypothesis. She admits she is impatient with herself and wants to be valedictorian. You seemed to have nailed the problem squarely on the head and are ready to dispute her unrealistic self-talk. You spend five sessions trying to whittle away at her overachieving standards and believe you are making progress. Then you receive a message on your answering machine from one of Tracy's concerned friends, saying, "I know I probably shouldn't be calling you, but I was afraid that Tracy hadn't told you she's bulimic." All of a sudden, your "overachieving theory" seems silly.

An effective counselor never jumps to conclusions. It is not easy to zero in on key issues in a session or two. Effective counselors are continually asking themselves, "Is there something else I may be missing?"

FEAR OF SILENCE

Counselors, especially in the beginning stages, are often afraid of silence. We feel a need to fill in the quiet gaps of communication. Silence, however, is not a signal that the counselor needs to say something. Silence is not a sign of doing something wrong. When you see the adolescent's wheels of thought and feeling turning, allow the process to happen without interruption. If a counselor is feeling nervous about silence, the results can be damaging. Interrupting clients before they have finished talking, cutting off productive thought, missing what clients are actually saying because you are mentally rehearsing what to say next, and so on, can all result from trying to avoid moments of silence.[2]

There are times, of course, when silence is not productive. Some young people, for example, may be socially anxious and for this reason simply do not talk much. Other teens will be naive about how therapy works and expect you to do all the talking. But more often, silence can be positive. Some of counseling's most therapeutic moments occur during periods of quiet contemplation. A teenager's deepest feeling will almost always reveal itself in silence. Counselors must remember that it takes clients much longer to incorporate what we have said than it took us to say it. Often, when clients are quiet they are doing their most important therapeutic work. Become comfortable with silence by maintaining eye contact with the young person and casually nod your head to convey your understanding and presence.[3]

INTERROGATING

Some counselors rely too much on asking questions—lots of questions. Learn to refrain from subjecting your client to an ongoing barrage of inquiries. Excessive probing can push a young person toward feeling "on the spot" or beleaguered. The result can be a superficial defensiveness. Information can be obtained without interrogation. For example, suppose a client says, "My father was angry at me for most of the afternoon." A natural line of questioning would be . . .

"How often does your father become angry?"
"What does he do when he is angry?"
"How does that make you feel?"

A therapist can obtain much of this information and more by saying something like, "I get the impression you have experienced your father's anger more than once." A statement like this lets the adolescent know he or she is understood and invites further disclosure without the risk of putting the client on the spot.

The skilled counselor can elicit information without a long list of questions. Actively trying to understand the client's experience helps him or her feel less defensive, and important information will become more readily available.

SETTING LIMITS

In an effort to be understanding and tolerant, some counselors have difficulty setting their own personal limits.[4] These limits include dealing appropriately with such issues as missed appointments or repeated calls on the phone by clients.

The amount of time you spend with teenagers in their sessions is another potential problem area. From time to time, a client may attempt to test your limits by continuing to talk past the appointed ending time of the session. Don't fall into this trap. Giving clients sixty or seventy minutes when you promised fifty, for example, may raise questions in the client's mind. Young people may wonder if you are strong enough to be their therapist if you cannot handle their end-of-session ramblings. Do not be afraid to set limits and hold to them. Adolescents, like all other clients, need stability and consistency in counseling.

MORALIZING

The counselor, like everyone else, has values, standards, and morals.[5] The profession of counseling does not require a therapist to compromise personal beliefs. However, professional counselors refrain from passing judgments on clients.[6] The therapeutic goal is to understand, not to condemn. Understanding, of course, does not of itself condone behavior. But a client can seldom be helped by a counselor who passes moral judgment. In fact, passing moral judgment, in the majority of cases, decreases the probability of healthy change.[7] Carl Rogers said, "When you criticize me, I intuitively dig in to defend myself. However, when you accept me like I am, I suddenly find I am willing to change."

IMPATIENCE

All therapists watch carefully for signs of progress. We want to see our clients improve—the sooner, the better. A counselor who is eager for this to happen, however, may subtly push unprepared clients into behavior before the time is right. Gradual change is not a reflection of poor therapy. Client readiness for genuine renewal or transformation takes time. A young person who is grieving the loss of a loved one, for example, cannot be forced to "snap out of it." A teenager struggling with an eating disorder cannot be expected to change her exercise and eating patterns radically over the course of a couple of weeks.

Young clients who are rushed into making rapid changes will be set up for further failure. Being "forced" to do something they are not adequately prepared for may result in extreme defensiveness, regression, or a premature termination of therapy altogether. Counselors must be sensitive to issues of personal impatience. Most young people cannot and will not make dramatic changes quickly.

RELUCTANCE TO REFER

Some counselors feel they are failing if they cannot meet the needs of every young person in pain. No counselor, however, is expected to work with every client who needs help. Beginning counselors must learn, early on, that referral to other competent counselors is a part of doing excellent therapeutic work. If for any reason—shortage of time, skill, or capacity to be emotionally present— you are not able to meet the needs of a client, referral is an ethical obligation.

Careful referral involves more than giving the client the name of another counselor. The client should be given a choice among therapists who are qualified to deal with the client's problems. And to protect against abandonment, the counselor can follow up on the referral to determine whether the appropriate contact was made. Each of the thirty "struggle" chapters in the accompanying volume to this book contains specific information on particular referral issues.

CONCLUSION

Fear of failure is one of the greatest obstacles counselors face. All therapists, regardless of experience and training, make mistakes. Even Freud, Rogers, Perls, Ellis, and all the other "experts" were not immune to blunders. If you are a counselor in training, give yourself permission to make mistakes and learn from them. No one expects you to be a "perfect" counselor right out of the gate. So don't give up if you initially fumble your way through the practice of counseling struggling adolescents.

The inventive genius Thomas Edison was faced one day with two dejected assistants, who told him, "We have just completed our seven hundredth experiment, and we still don't have a light bulb. We have failed."

"We haven't failed," said Edison. "We have made progress. Now we know seven hundred things not to do. We are becoming experts." Edison then told his colleagues, "With each 'mistake,' we are one step closer to reaching our goal."

Edison's wisdom makes sense in learning how to counsel. It is hoped that you will avoid the mistakes summarized in this chapter and will journey closer to the quality of effectiveness, but you are certain to stumble from time to time. Someone has said that if Thomas Edison had given up easily, you and I would be watching television in the dark. Discussing your self-doubts with colleagues or a supervisor takes courage, but it will bring you closer to your goal of becoming an effective therapist of teenagers who need your help.

Notes

1. Combs, A. (1986). What makes a good helper. *Person-Centered Review, 1,* 51–61.

2. Brams, J. (1961). Counselor characteristics and effective communication in counseling. *Journal of Counseling Psychology, 8,* 25–30.

3. Barrett-Lennard, G. T. (1962). Dimensions of therapist response as causal factors in therapeutic change. *Psychological Monographs, 76* (43, Whole no. 562).

4. Allen, T. (1967). Effectiveness of counselor trainees as a function of psychological openness. *Journal of Counseling Psychology, 14,* 35–40.

5. Sue, D. W. (1978). World views and counseling. *Personnel and Guidance Journal, 56,* 458–62.

6. Williamson, E. (1958). Value orientation in counseling. *Personnel and Guidance Journal, 36,* 520–28.

7. Patterson, C. (1958). The place of values in counseling and psychotherapy. *Journal of Counseling Psychology, 5,* 216–23.

2

Legal and Ethical Issues
Related to Counseling

During the first half of construction on the Golden Gate Bridge in San Francisco, some twenty men fell from their work to their death or to serious injury. Finally construction was stopped and a giant net built under the work area so anyone who fell subsequently would be caught. During the remaining construction, only four men fell. The net not only made the workers feel safe, but also made them more confident and less likely to fall.

Professional counselors can work with the same confidence and protect their therapeutic practice from tumbling by using the "net" of legal and ethical guidelines. These protective measures make counseling safe for therapists as well as clients.

Few professions can match the intensity and consequences of the everyday ethical dilemmas psychotherapists face. There have been numerous volumes written about legal and ethical issues for counselors. This chapter, however, will lift out and briefly discuss only the most common legal and ethical concerns pertaining to counseling.

FOUNDATIONS OF LEGAL AND ETHICAL PRACTICE

A young priest saw a vision of God in a great cathedral. He ran to the bishop and, gasping for breath, cried out, "I have just seen a vision of God. He's behind that pillar over there. What should we do?"

The bishop said, "Quick! Look busy!"

The foundations of legal and ethical practice are not formed by "looking" legal or "appearing" ethical. A legal and ethical counseling practice is grounded on something you *are*, not something you *do*. The bedrock of legal and ethical counseling is *virtue*—a term rarely heard in psychology.[1] Virtue should not be confused with a principle or rule; "rather, it is a habit, disposition, or trait that a person may possess or aspire to possess. A moral virtue is an acquired habit or disposition to do what is morally right or praiseworthy."[2]

The virtuous counselor, however, does not acquire ethical behavior through good intentions. He or she begins with being legally and ethically competent. One's practice is built on knowing the law and understanding client rights.[3] His or her virtue is nourished by being rooted in (1) a solid knowledge of the law, (2) firm ethical standards of the profession, and (3) stable personal morals, values, and beliefs.

The idea of *virtue ethics* focuses on *being* as much as on *doing*. Virtuous counselors emphasize "not so much what is permitted as what is preferred."[4] The personal values of the counselor can serve as a basis for empowering the practice of ethical behavior. A counselor's ethical behavior involves more than subscribing to a code of ethics. A heartfelt responsibility to relate behavior to ethics is crucial.[5] Good ethics are built on a genuine concern for the client's welfare.[6]

Legally, the therapist must—

- Possess the degree of learning, skill, and ability that others similarly situated ordinarily possess;
- Exercise reasonable care and diligence in the application of knowledge and skill to the patient's case; and
- Use one's best judgment in the treatment and care of a patient.[7]

Counselors must be clear and honest with themselves about the limits of their own expertise.[8] The American Psychological Association requires professionals to "provide services and only use techniques for which they are qualified by training and experience."[9] Being competent as a therapist does not mean being able to treat every person who needs counseling. A responsible therapist will only accept clients who can benefit from the training and skill the therapist has acquired. Research has shown that inexpert counseling can indeed be worse than no treatment at all.[10] Competency means knowing what issues you cannot treat because you are not qualified by training and experience.

Simply reading a book or attending a weekend workshop devoted to a particular topic does not qualify a counselor to begin unsupervised experience in a new area of treatment. If a counselor wishes to expand an area of professional competence, supervision from a clearly qualified professional is essential.

Failure to practice at a reasonable level of competence may result in being sued for damage due to malpractice. Generally, malpractice is defined as "a failure to meet prevailing, professionally accepted standards of practice."[11] Counselors have an obligation to their clients and to their profession to be accountable for the quality of the professional services they offer.

A counselor who recognizes that a client's needs are beyond his or her expertise is responsible to make referrals to other competent counselors. When making referrals, counselors should help clients understand the reasons for the referral and the distinctive qualifications of the professional to whom the referral is made. If, for example, a counselor is referring a client to a psychiatrist, the counselor should explain that a psychiatrist is practicing a medical specialty and that a psychiatrist may prescribe medication for psychological problems.[12]

THE CLIENT-COUNSELOR RELATIONSHIP

Trust is the essence of a therapeutic relationship. Counseling young people deals with deeply personal issues and requires a high level of risk-taking on the part of teens. Without a reasonable level of trust, a therapeutic relationship can never occur. Counselor effectiveness is proportionate to the amount of trustworthiness established with clients. As trust is diminished, so is effectiveness.

Informed consent is the basis of a trusting relationship and a cornerstone of counselor ethics. Through informed consent, clients are told what can be expected during treatment, how long it may take, and how much it will cost. They are also informed of their right to agree or decline to participate in any aspect of counseling. The information is communicated, not in psychobabble and jargon, but in language that is easily understood. Responsible informed consent also gives clients opportunities to ask questions. A therapist should "describe the therapeutic program recommended, indicating also the anticipated benefits of the program, the foreseeable material risks of treatment, and the likely results of no treatment."[13]

Counselors are responsible for providing the following information to clients at the outset of counseling:

1. A description of his or her role and qualifications as a counselor
2. An explanation of the process of counseling and any particular procedures or approaches to be used, and their purpose
3. A description of any discomfort or risks that may evolve
4. A description of any reasonably expected benefits
5. A disclosure of other approaches or strategies that may also be useful
6. An offer to answer inquiries about counseling or procedures at any time
7. A statement that the client can withdraw consent and discontinue participation in a procedure or in therapy at any time[14]

Psychotherapists continue to battle the mistaken notion that therapists have "magical" powers—that therapists are latter-day soothsayers. Much of the public must be educated regarding the realities of counseling. Some professionals call for an ethical obligation to dispel erroneous thinking about counseling. "Therapists should attempt to create reasonable expectations for the public about what psychotherapy can and cannot do. Perhaps a return to Freud's goal of ordinary human misery is called for, rather than our current pursuit of wrinkle-free, drip-dry, perfectible man."[15]

What about associating with clients outside of the therapeutic setting? "Deep down in his mind," according to Frieda Fromm-Reichmann, "no patient wants a nonprofessional relationship with his therapist, regardless of the fact that he may express himself to the contrary."[16] Some believe that a relationship with a client outside of the therapeutic context will almost always complicate treatment.[17] It can lead to a tangled web of dual or multiple roles. To protect the welfare of clients, counselors must work to avoid dual relationships. Otherwise, they will run the risk of clouding objectivity and interfering with the therapeutic process. Dual relationships also increase the probability of the kinds of sexual intimacies in psychotherapy that often receive wide publicity.[18]

CONFIDENTIALITY AND PRIVILEGED INFORMATION

A fourteen-year-old told his inexperienced counselor, "Look, I need your help. Can I tell you a secret without you telling anyone else?"

Sensing something serious and wanting the adolescent to open up, the new counselor agreed to keep quiet.

"My dad is a total jerk, and I can't handle it any more. I got a ticket to California, and I'm gone, man. I want you to give me a week and then give my mom this." The teenager handed over two folded sheets of white notebook paper, stapled shut.

The counselor tried to change the boy's mind or get him to at least talk to his father first. He offered to mediate the conversation, but the boy stood firm and finally left.

Even though he had agreed not to break the secret, the counselor wondered whether he shouldn't tell someone. He thought that breaking a confidence equaled sin, but he continued to wrestle with his conscience.

Problems of confidentiality are the most common source of ethical dilemmas for counselors.[19] Confidentiality can be defined by a relationship built on trust in which a client reveals private or secret information to a counselor. Confidentiality assumes that the counselor, "having grown powerful as a result of such knowledge, discloses the information to others only at the behest or with the consent of the the [client]."[20] This means that counselors do not talk to anyone about a client or even reveal that they are seeing a client without prior permission from a client.[21]

There is no justifiable excuse for inadvertent slips that reveal information shared in confidence. Even nondamaging information is to be protected. "Any information obtained in professional relationships is to be treated confidentially."[22] Clients deserve to have their personal information protected by strict confidentiality. Then they can be free of worry over who might hear the private information they discuss. Confidentiality protects clients from having their counselors "gossip" about them. It is a keystone of therapy.[23]

Confidentiality does have limits, however;[24] it is an ethical principle rather than a legal one. Confidentiality involves "professional ethics rather than any legalism and indicates an explicit promise or contract to reveal nothing about an individual except under conditions agreed to by the source or subject."[25] In legal terms, the concept of confidentiality is known as privileged communication. The law spells out the legal conditions for breaking confidence with a client.[26] Privileged communication has been defined as "the legal right which exists by statute and which protects the client from having his confidences revealed publicly from the witness stand during legal proceedings without his permission."[27] Lawyers, physicians, ministers, and psychologists are among the few professionals who have a legal right to claim privileged information.

Ethical dilemmas such as the case of the fourteen-year-old cited earlier also arise because of a conflict between what is best for the client and what is best for other people. "When a counselor encourages a client to believe that a communication will be held in full and complete confidence, the only ethical ground for breaking that confidence is danger to human life."[28] In other words, privileged communication does not hold up in cases where the counselor has reasonable cause to believe that the person is in such a psychological state as to be dangerous to himself or to the person or property of another. For example, health and mental health professionals have a duty to warn the sexual partners of clients with AIDS if the clients refuse to do so themselves.[29]

In such cases, counselors have a "duty to warn" by disclosing information that can prevent a threatened danger.[30] A confidence should be broken when (1) the client is in danger to himself or others, (2) the client is engaged in criminal actions, (3) the counselor is so ordered by the court, or (4) it is in the best interests of a child who is a victim of abuse.[31]

A famous case illustrates the importance of disclosing information that can prevent harmful results. In August 1969 a college student, Prosejit Poddar, informed his counselor that he was planning to kill his girlfriend, Tatiana Tarasoff. Poddar was a voluntary outpatient at the Cowell Memorial Hospital on the Berkeley campus of the University of California. The therapist later called the campus police and told them of this threat. He asked the campus police to observe Poddar and watch for danger signs that might require psychiatric hospitalization.

The campus officers did take Poddar into custody for questioning, but they later released him because he was "rational." Poddar's counselor followed up his telephone call with a formal letter requesting the assistance of the chief of the campus police. Later, the counselor's supervisor asked that the letter be returned, ordered that the letter and the therapist's case notes be destroyed, and asked that no further action be taken in the case. No warning of Tatiana's peril was given to either the intended viction or her parents.

Two months later, on 27 October 1969, Poddar killed Tatiana Tarasoff. In what is now a landmark court case referred to as the Tarasoff decision, Tatiana Tarasoff's parents filed suit against the Board of Regents and employees of the university for failing to notify the intended victim of the threat. A lower court dismissed the suit; the parents appealed; and the California Supreme Court ruled in favor of the parents in 1976 and held that a failure to warn the intended victim was irresponsible.

This case resulted in the enactment of laws requiring psychotherapists to warn individuals when they become aware of intentions to harm: "We conclude that the public policy favoring protection of the confidential character of patient-psychotherapist communication must yield to the extent that exposure is essential to avert danger to others. The protection privilege ends where the public peril begins."[32]

Clients should be apprised of the limits of confidentiality at the outset of therapy. Counselors should also obtain client permission before tape-recording a session or sharing information with a supervisor.[33] Of course, supervisors, like counselors, are obligated to respect the confidentiality of client communication. "When a clear policy exists and is explained to the client before confidences are accepted, many ethical and professional problems can be avoided."[34]

WHEN IN DOUBT . . .

I am sorry to say that I have seen fine counselors stumble professionally because they did not use accessible resources for understanding and practicing the legal and ethical standards of counseling, namely, consultation with other colleagues.

When in doubt, consult a colleague. Legal and ethical considerations can be complex and confusing. Effective counselors consult regularly with other professionals on issues that are unclear. This consultation can take the form of a brief phone call or be as extensive as bringing in a colleague to supervise your sessions. Counselors can also obtain guidance by phone from state and national counseling organizations such as the American Counseling Association and the American Psychological Association.

In addition to consulting with professional colleagues, competent counselors will also commonly make referrals to other counselors who can meet the needs of a particular client more effectively. A referral may be necessary when the following situations arise:

- Your client wishes to pursue matters that are contrary to professional ethics, legal codes, or your value system
- You lack essential knowledge or skills for the best modes of treatment for a particular client
- Personality differences between you and the client prevent working together effectively
- Interpersonal connections with the client outside of counseling might create a conflict of interest (e.g., being asked to counsel a family member of an associate)
- You and your client are making little progress toward treatment goals, and prospects for making greater progress are dim.[35]

It is also a good idea to refer a person for a thorough physical examination as part of the counseling evaluation. In addition, it can sometimes be important to enlist the aid of a minister, especially when the young person communicates a need for spiritual comfort during crisis interventions. A referral to a counselor of the same sex can be helpful in allowing a client to feel more comfortable. A young woman who has just broken up with her boyfriend, for example, may feel more comfortable and do better therapeutic work with a female therapist. For more information on referral issues related to specific adolescent struggles, see the companion volume to this book.

Both the American Psyschological Association and the American Counseling Association have published detailed ethical guidelines for their members (APA, 1990; AACD, 1988). The documents should be consulted by any practitioner who is in doubt about specific ethical questions.

Notes

1. Gelso, C. J., and Fretz, B. R. (1992). *Counseling psychology*. Fort Worth: Harcourt Brace Jovanovich.

2. Beauchamp, T. L., and Childress, J. S. (1983). *Principles of biomedical ethics* (2d ed.). New York: Oxford University Press, p. 261.

3. Hatton, C. L., Balente, S. M., and Rink, A. (1977). *Suicide: Assessment and intervention.* Englewood Cliffs, NJ: Prentice-Hall.

4. Jordan, A. E., and Meara, N. M. (1990). Ethics and the professional practice of psychologists: The role of virtues and principles. *Professional Psychology Research and Practice, 21,* 107–14, p. 112.

5. Wrenn, C. G. (1958). Psychology, religion, and values for the counselor, Part III, in the symposium, the counselor and his religion. *Personnel and Guidance Journal, 36,* 326–34.

6. Corey, G., Corey, M. S., and Callanan, P. (1992). *Issues and ethics in the helping professions* (4th ed.). Pacific Grove, CA: Brooks/Cole.

7. Furrow, B. R. (1980). *Malpractice in psychotherapy.* Lexington, MA: Lexington Books, p. 23.

8. Pope, K. S., and Vasquez, M. J. T. (1991). *Ethics in psychotherapy and counseling: A practical guide for psychologists.* San Francisco: Jossey-Bass.

9. American Psychological Association (1990). Ethical principles of psychologists. *American Psychologist, 45,* 390–95.

10. Bergin, A. E. (1963). The effects of psychotherapy: Negative effects revisited. *Journal of Counseling Psychology, 10,* 244–49.

11. Blocher, D. H. (1987). *The professional counselor.* New York: Macmillan, p. 30.

12. Cormier, W. H., and Cormier, L. S. (1991). *Interviewing strategies for helpers* (3d ed.). Monterey, CA: Brooks/Cole.

13. Schutz, B. (1982). *Legal liability in psychotherapy.* San Francisco: Jossey-Bass, p. 24.

14. Cormier, L. S., and Hackney, H. (1987). *The professional counselor: A process guide to helping.* Englewood Cliffs, NJ: Prentice-Hall.

15. Schutz, B. (1982), p. 95.

16. Frieda Fromm-Reichmann (1950).

17. Borys, D. S., and Pope, K. S. (1989). Dual relationships between therapist and client: A national study of psychologists, psychiatrists, and social workers. *Professional Psychology: Research and Practice, 20,* 283–93.

18. Williams, M. H. (1992). Exploitation and inference: Mapping the damage from therapist-patient sexual involvement. *American Psychologist, 47,* 412–21; and Pope, K. S. (1990). Therapist-patient sexual involvement: A review of the research. *Clinical Psychology Review, 10,* 477–90.

19. Pope, K. S., and Vetter, V. A. (1992). Ethical dilemmas encountered by members of the American Psychological Association. *American Psychologist, 47,* 397–411.

20. Dulchin, J., and Segal, A. J. (1982). The ambiguity of confidentiality in a psychoanalytic institute. *Psychiatry, 45,* 13–25, p. 13.

21. Knapp, S., and VandeCreek, L. (1987). *Privileged communications in the mental health professions.* New York: Van Nostrand Reinhold.

22. Gelso, C. J., and Fretz, B. R. (1992), p. 56.

23. Sheeley, V. L., and Herlihy, B. (1986). The ethics of confidentiality and privileged communication. *Journal of Counseling and Human Service Professions, 1*, 141–48.

24. Denkowski, K. M., and Denkowski, G. C. (1982). Client-counselor confidentiality: An update of rationale, legal status, and implications. *Personnel and Guidance Journal, 60*, 371–75.

25. Siegel, M. (1979). Privacy, ethics and confidentiality. *Professional Psychology, 10*, 249–58, p. 251.

26. DeKraai, M. B., and Sales, B. D. (1982). Confidential communications of psychotherapists. *Psychotherapy, 21*, 293–318. Herlihy, B., and Sheeley, B. L. (1987). Privileged communication in selected helping professions: A comparison among statutes. *Journal of Counseling and Development, 65*, 479–83.

27. Shah, S. (1969). Privileged communications, confidentiality, and privacy: Privileged communications. *Professional Psychology, 1*, 56–69, p. 57.

28. Blocher (1987).

29. Cohen, E. D. (1990). Confidentiality, counseling, and clients who have AIDS: Ethical foundations of a model rule. *Journal of Counseling and Development, 68*, 282–86; Lamb, D. H., et al. (1989). Applying Tarasoff to AIDS-related psychotherapy issues. *Professional Psychology: Research and Practice, 20*, 37–43.

30. Gehring, D. D. (1982). The counselor's "duty to warn." *Personnel and Guidance Journal, 61*, 208–10; and Leslie, R. (1983). Tarasoff decision extended. *California Therapist*, Nov./Dec., p. 6.

31. Berger, M. (1982). Ethics and the therapeutic relationship. In M. Rosenbaum (Ed.), *Ethics and values in psychotherapy*, pp. 67–95. New York: Free Press.

32. Beauchamp and Childress (1983), p. 283.

33. McGuire, J. M., Graves, S., and Blau, B. (1985). Depth of self-disclosure as a function of assured confidentiality and videotape recording. *Journal of Counseling and Development, 64*, 259–63.

34. Blocher (1987), p. 26.

35. MacDonald, D. (1992). *Making effective referrals.* Unpublished manuscript.

3

Avoiding Counselor Burnout: A Survival Kit

You may have heard the tongue-in-cheek story of the man who was about to jump from a bridge. A counselor, driving home from a long day of work, spotted him. Slowly and methodically the counselor moved toward the man. When he was within inches of him, the counselor said, "Surely nothing could be bad enough for you to take your life. Tell me about it." The would-be jumper told how he worked hard but saw few results and got little recognition, how his days had become robotic, how he didn't find time to do what really mattered, and how life had lost its meaning. The counselor listened to the sad story for thirty minutes. Then they both jumped!

Counseling *is* difficult. At times it is discouraging. Burnout is the consequence for counselors who do not have a strategic plan to cope with the emotional stresses that come from continued intimate work with troubled human beings—many of whom do not get better. This chapter offers practical means to prevent burnout and to help you cope with the inevitable frustrations that are a natural part of working with struggling adolescents.

WHAT IS BURNOUT?

Once sensitive, caring, and vibrant with enthusiasm, Jim seems to have lost the joy he once had in counseling teenagers. He doesn't admit it to others, but now he doesn't even care about the adolescents who come to see him. At times he even catches himself about to express his anger and frustration at them. The people in Jim's life have noticed a difference too. He seems far away, not so much fun anymore. Jim has the classic symptoms of burnout: feelings of futility, powerlessness, fatigue, cynicism, apathy, irritability, and frustration.

Burnout is a response to repeated emotional strain. One researcher has described the process of burnout in four stages: enthusiasm, stagnation, frustration, and apathy.[1]

Several basic characteristics have been specifically associated with burned-out counselors: They have lost concern for the people they counsel; they have become detached from the people around them; they have become cynical and even blame counselees for the counselees' own problems; and they have become emotionally frustrated and sometimes complain of psychosomatic ailments.[2]

Counselors are particularly susceptible to burnout because they are involved in emotionally taxing work. They also tend to be sensitive to others' problems and have a desire to relieve suffering. Additionally, counselors often see their work as a calling to be givers to those who feel powerless and helpless.[3] Their focus is often on taking care of others, not themselves. Without a strategic plan to avoid frustration, fatigue, and disillusionment, counselors are walking along the rim of a deep chasm.

CAUSES OF BURNOUT

According to one study, two predominant factors cause burnout: "lack of therapeutic success, and nonreciprocated giving that is required of the counseling relationship."[4] Although other factors—an excessive work load, professional isolation, personal problems, and so on—will obviously lower the burnout threshold, it is lack of success and the absence of appreciation that tends to throw most counselors over the edge.

Although counselors expect their work to be difficult and even stressful, they do not expect their work to fail or go unnoticed. Counselors expect to see positive results and to have their efforts appreciated. These latter expectations plant the seeds that lead to burnout.

A BURNOUT CHECKLIST

Review the past twelve months of your total life: work, social situations, family, and recreation. Reflect on each question in the following exercise and rate the amount of change that has occurred during the past six months. Use the scale to assign a number in the rating column that reflects the degree of change you have experienced.[5]

A Burnout Checklist

1 = Little or no change
2 = Barely noticeable change
3 = Readily noticeable change
4 = A fair degree of change
5 = A great degree of change

___ 1. Do you become more fatigued, tired, or "worn out" by the end of the day?

___ 2. Have you lost interest in your present work?

___ 3. Have you lost ambition in your overall career?

___ 4. Do you become easily bored (spending long hours with nothing significant to do)?

___ 5. Have you become more pessimistic or cynical in your relationship to yourself or others?

___ 6. Do you forget appointments, deadlines, or activities and not feel very concerned about it?

___ 7. Do you spend more time alone, withdrawn from friends, family, and work acquaintances?

___ 8. Do you become irritable, hostile, or aggressive more often?

___ 9. Has your sense of humor become less obvious to you or others?

___10. Do you become sick more easily (flu, colds, pain problems)?

___11. Do you experience headaches more than usual?

___12. Do you suffer from gastrointestinal problems (stomach pains, chronic diarrhea, or colitis)?

___13. Do you wake up feeling extremely tired and exhausted more often?

___14. Do you deliberately try to avoid people you previously did not mind being around?

___15. Has there been a lessening of your sexual drive?

___16. Do you now tend to treat people as "impersonal objects" or with a fair degree of callousness?

___17. Do you feel that you are not accomplishing anything worthwhile in your work and that you are ineffective in making any changes?

___18. Do you feel that you are not accomplishing anything worthwhile in your personal life or that you have lost spontaneity in your activities?

___19. Do you spend much time each day thinking or worrying about your job, people, future, or past?

___20. Do you feel that you are at the "end of your tether"—that you are at the point of "breaking down" or "cracking up"?

___ *Total Score*

Your score on this checklist is merely a guide to your experience of burnout.

20–30	There is no burnout. You may be taking your life or work too casually.
31–45	This is a normal score for anyone who works hard and seriously.
46–60	You are experiencing some mild burnout and could benefit from a careful review of your lifestyle.
61–75	You are beginning to experience burnout. Take action to get better control of your life.

76–90   You are burning out. Seek help, reevaluate your life, and make changes.

91–100   You are dangerously burned out and need immediate relief. Your burnout is threatening your physical and mental well-being.

A SURVIVAL KIT FOR COUNSELORS

The first step in staying alive as a counselor to struggling adolescents is to admit the existence of danger in your work. Adolescents are, for many, the most frustrating group of people to work with in a counseling setting. In an effort to develop personal identity, adolescents often resist help and show little improvement. Also, it is rare for struggling adolescents to recognize and appreciate counselors' patient work. Don't bank on receiving compliments from hurting teenagers. If counselors are to survive as healthy human beings, they must have a strategic plan, a survival kit, to guard against the ravages of emotional burnout.

Owning Responsibility Prevents Burnout

Many counselors who are teetering on the edge of burnout blame the system and other external factors for their condition. They say things like, "I have too many demands on my time, and I feel useless because I just can't meet them all." Or, "Adolescents resist help and they just don't want to change. That's why I feel like a failure." Statements like these place the responsibility outside of the counselor—as if some force is making us ineffective. In this passive stance, we increase the likelihood of our falling into the chasm of burnout. The more we blame external factors, the more we surrender personal power. Despite external realities that take their toll on our energy, we must recognize and accept our part in allowing ourselves to burn out. We must shift our focus away from what we cannot do and channel our energy toward changes that are within our control.

Community Prevents Burnout

We need a compassionate community that will confront us when the burnout monster begins to raise its head. Few counselors take the initiative to recognize that burnout is beginning to control them. Such recognition invariably is in response to another's caring concern. If we are to survive, we must have people in our lives who care enough about us to hold up the mirror of reality that reflects our feelings of futility, irritability, and apathy.

Realistic Expectations Prevent Burnout

Don't measure your work against those who are able to do more with less effort. No matter how long and hard you work, there will always be others who put more of themselves into projects. They seem always to look forward to the next assignment. Some come out of difficult situations with an adrenaline rush,

Keys to Preventing Counselor Burnout

- Find an activity that diverts your attention away from work—something that makes you forget what you do for a living.
- Put some variety into your daily routine. Counselors most susceptible to burnout limit their work to one type of activity.
- Balance your life with the basic ingredients of a healthful lifestyle: adequate sleep, exercise, and proper diet.
- Set limits with demanding counselees and stick to them. It is possible to be both assertive and affirming at the same time.
- Rely on prayer to guard you from negative self-talk. God will keep you in "perfect peace" when your mind is stayed on him (Isa. 26:3).
- Have something at your office that is just for fun. I know a counselor who juggles between each session.
- Express to colleagues your frustrations resulting from work with adolescents (rather than keeping the frustrations to yourself).
- Rearrange or redecorate your office. A change in your environment will help keep you from becoming stale.
- Take time off to escape and seek new experiences through travel. Diversion helps to replenish personal resources and restore meaning to work.
- Practice a relaxation technique regularly.
- Cultivate your sense of humor. Some counselors adopt a somber attitude toward life and forget how to laugh.

feeling energized and excited. Others come away feeling drained. Comparing yourself to others may set you up for a good case of depression and burnout. As one of my counselees told me recently, "When I compare myself to the way Julie gets her work done, I feel as if I'm sculpting in the same room with Michelangelo."

Authentic Spirituality Prevents Burnout

A genuine and active spiritual life, motivated by love not guilt, increases our awareness of God's healing work in the counseling setting. It deepens our dependence on him to bring about true therapeutic change. His strength is made perfect in our weakness (2 Cor. 12:9). When anxious and distressed about approaching the threshold of burnout, counselors who have a relationship with God will avail themselves of psychological and physical interventions, but they will also call on the strength they find in the love of Christ. Jesus, as the great shepherd, loves and cares for his sheep. As we allow him to shepherd our work with struggling adolescents, he restores our souls (Ps. 23).

A Final Comment on Burnout

This brief chapter is designed to help counselors keep from slipping into burnout. It has said little about what to do if you have already fallen in.[6] While burnout is often overcome through changes in lifestyle, there are times when professional help is needed. If you are in a state of emotional turmoil, extreme fatigue, negativism, depression, and isolation, you probably need psychotherapy. Burnout may be the consequence of underlying issues, and self-help in severe cases will only exacerbate the symptoms. Professional therapy may be a useful source of reconstitution for the severely burned-out counselor.

Notes

1. Edelwich, J. (1980). *Burnout: Stages of disillusionment in the helping professions*. New York: Human Sciences Press.

2. Farber, B. A., and Heifetz, L. J. (1982). The process and dimensions of burnout in psychotherapists. *Professional Psychology, 13* (2), 293–301.

3. Pines, A., and Aronson, E., with Dafry, D. (1981). *Burnout: From tedium to personal growth*. New York: Free Press.

4. Farber and Heifetz (1982).

5. Hart, A. D. (March 1984). Test yourself: Burnout checklist, *Theology News and Notes*, p. 4.

6. For more specific help for recovery from burnout, I recommend the following resources: *Burnout in ministry* by Brooks R. Faulkner, Nashville: Broadman; *Depression in ministry and the helping professions* by Archibald D. Hart, Waco, TX: Word Books (1984); *Burnout—The cost of caring* by Christina Maslach, Englewood Cliffs, NJ: Prentice-Hall (1982); and *When helping you is hurting me* by Carmen Berry, San Francisco: Harper & Row (1986).

Part Two

Rapid Assessment Tools

Using and Interpreting
Rapid Assessment Tools

Most counselors agree that without some form of assessment, attempts to help are aimless. It is analogous to a physician's asking a patient with a fractured arm, "Where is it broken?" without bothering to take an X-ray. Assessment tools give the counselor a clearer picture of a person's struggle. They help us begin to answer the when, why, where, and how questions and to ascertain to what degree the person struggles. They guard us against projecting our partial and less quantifiable evaluations onto the adolescent; they help us view a situation with objectivity.

Another valuable feature of these assessment tools is that they allow us to track the successes (and failures) of our therapeutic work. By readministering the tool, we can objectively answer the question, "How are you doing compared with three months ago when you first came to see me?"

For these reasons, this handbook provides dozens of paper-and-pencil instruments that can assist you in counseling adolescents who have a variety of struggles. Each tool was selected because of its simplicity. They are quick (requiring no more than a few minutes' work) and easy to administer, score, and interpret.

INTERPRETING THE TOOLS: A WORD OF CAUTION

The purpose of rapid assessment tools is to help counselors monitor and evaluate their progress in working with young people. While these tools can be useful to counselors who have little experience in using assessment instruments, these tests have many limitations. Be cautious—rapid assessment tools are not a panacea. Results from each of these tests are only estimates. These tests do not measure the many nuances of a particular struggle, and in some cases they may be misleading. Since even very sophisticated assessment instruments are not completely reliable or valid, you must be judicious about accepting scores as "truth." Moreover, scores always contain some measurement error, which means decisions about your counseling practice can be incorrect if based strictly on a rapid assessment tool.

Most rapid assessment tools are based on face validity or content validity, and test results can easily be affected by the test-taking stance of the young person. For example, a child taking the CAT–F might be reluctant to admit negative feelings about the father and so would under-report problems by distorting the truth.

Another word of caution: Most of these measures have been used primarily with a white, middle-class American population. For this reason you must use extreme care if you are administering these instruments to young people from other ethnic or socioeconomic groups.

Rapid assessment tools are far from perfect. But when used widely in the context of the entire therapeutic relationship, they can be valuable to counselors working with struggling adolescents.

List of Instruments Cross-referenced by Problem Area

Anger
Anger Situations Form   *41*
Novaco Anger Scale   *110*
State-Trait Anger Scale   *141*
Anxiety
Clinical Anxiety Scale   *59*
Stressors Rating Scale   *144*
Self-Rating Anxiety Scale   *125*
Body Image
Compulsive Eating Scale   *64*
Internal Versus External Control of Weight Scale   *101*
Decision Making
Checklist for Making a Major Decision   *52*
Depression
Dysfunctional Attitude Scale   *73*
Generalized Contentment Scale   *87*
Self-Rating Depression Scale   *127*
Drugs and Alcohol
Michigan Alcoholism Screening Test   *105*
Teen Alert Questionnaire   *147*
Eating Disorders
Are You Dying To Be Thin? Scale   *43*
Bulimia Test   *46*
Concern Over Weight and Dieting Scale   *69*
Eating Attitudes Test   *76*
Goldfarb Fear of Fat Scale   *89*
Restraint Scale   *118*
Forgiveness
Novaco Anger Scale   *110*
Guilt
Guilt Scale   *91*

Anger Situations Form (ASF)

Chapter Link

This form is to be used in conjunction with the Anger chapter of *Helping the Struggling Adolescent*.

Rapid Assessment Description

This brief form is designed to identify the individuals and the situations that exacerbate a young person's feelings of anger.

Scoring Procedure

This form is not scored. It is simply used to locate who and what may be involved in a young person's anger. The form can serve as a springboard for discussions focusing on the young person's angry feelings.

Permission

The ASF is available from Research Press, 2612 North Mattis Avenue, Champaign, IL 61821. Copyright © 1990 by Rosemarie S. Morganett. Reprinted by permission.

ASF

Instructions: Put a checkmark in the appropriate box to show the people and situations that are involved in your anger.

Situations	Mom	Dad	Sister	People Brother	Friend	Teacher	Other	Other
Not getting what I want	☐	☐	☐	☐	☐	☐	☐	☐
Unfair treatment	☐	☐	☐	☐	☐	☐	☐	☐
Loss (friendship, opportunity, etc.)	☐	☐	☐	☐	☐	☐	☐	☐
Fights	☐	☐	☐	☐	☐	☐	☐	☐
Disrespect	☐	☐	☐	☐	☐	☐	☐	☐
Dishonesty	☐	☐	☐	☐	☐	☐	☐	☐
Other	☐	☐	☐	☐	☐	☐	☐	☐
Other	☐	☐	☐	☐	☐	☐	☐	☐

Are You Dying To Be Thin? (ADT)

Chapter Link

This scale is to be used in conjunction with the Eating Disorders chapter of *Helping the Struggling Adolescent.*

Rapid Assessment Description

This questionnaire is designed to reveal whether or not a person thinks or behaves in ways that indicate tendencies toward anorexia nervosa or bulimia nervosa.

Scoring Procedure

Add scores from each of the items and compare the total score with the following table:

38 or less	Strong tendencies toward anorexia nervosa.
39–50	Strong tendencies toward bulimia nervosa.
51–60	Weight conscious. May or may not have tendencies toward an eating disorder. Not likely to have anorexia or bulimia nervosa. May have tendencies toward compulsive eating or obesity.
Over 60	Extremely unlikely to have anorexia or bulimia nervosa. However, scoring over 60 does not rule out tendencies toward compulsive eating or obesity.

Permission

The ADT is reprinted by permission of Kim Lampson-Reif, Ph.D. Copyright © 1989.

Available from K. Kim Lampson-Reif, Ph.D., Sherwood Forest Office Park, 2661 Bel-Red Road, Suite 104, Bellevue, WA 98008.

ADT

Answer the questions below honestly. Respond as you are now, not the way you used to be or the way you would like to be. Write the letter of your answer in the space at the left. Do not leave any questions blank unless instructed to do so.

_____ 1. I have eating habits that are different from those of my family and friends.
      a. Often   b. Sometimes   c. Rarely   d. Never

_____ 2. I find myself panicking if I cannot exercise as I planned because I am afraid I will gain weight if I don't.
      a. Often   b. Sometimes   c. Rarely   d. Never

_____ 3. My friends tell me I am thin, but I don't believe them because I feel fat.
      a. Often   b. Sometimes   c. Rarely   d. Never

_____ 4. (Females only) My menstrual period has stopped or become irregular due to no known medical reason.
      a. True   b. False

_____ 5. I have become obsessed with food to the point that I cannot go through a day without worrying about what I will or will not eat.
      a. Almost always   b. Sometimes   c. Rarely   d. Never

_____ 6. I have lost more than 15 percent of what is considered a healthy weight for my height (e.g., female, 5'4" tall, healthy weight=122 lbs., lost 20 lbs.) and currently weigh that weight or less.
      a. True   b. False

_____ 7. I would panic if I got on the scale tomorrow and found out I had gained two pounds.
      a. Almost always   b. Sometimes   c. Rarely   d. Never

_____ 8. I find that I prefer to eat alone or when I am sure no one will see me and thus make excuses so I can eat less and less with friends and family.
      a. Often   b. Sometimes   c. Rarely   d. Never

_____ 9. I find myself going on uncontrollable eating binges during which I consume large amounts of food to the point that I feel sick and make myself vomit.
      a. Never   b. Less than 1 time per week
      c. 1-6 times per week   d. 1 or more times per day

_____10. (*Note: Answer only if your response to no. 9 is "a"; otherwise leave blank.*) I find myself compulsively eating more than I want to while feeling out of control and/or unaware of what I am doing.
      a. Never   b. Less than 1 time per week
      c. 1-6 times per week   d. 1 or more times per day

_____11. I use laxatives or diuretics as a means of weight control.
      a. Never   b. Rarely   c. Sometimes   d. On a regular basis

____12. I find myself playing games with food (e.g., cutting it into tiny pieces, hiding food so people will think I ate it, chewing it and spitting it out without swallowing it, keeping hidden stashes of food) and/or telling myself certain foods are bad.
a. Often   b. Sometimes   c. Rarely   d. Never

____13. People around me have become very interested in what I eat, and I find myself getting angry toward them for pushing me to eat more.
a. Often   b. Sometimes   c. Rarely   d. Never

____14. I have felt more depressed and irritable recently than I used to and/or have been spending an increasing amount of time alone.
a. True   b. False

____15. I keep a lot of my fears about food and eating to myself because I am afraid no one would understand.
a. Often   b. Sometimes   c. Rarely   d. Never

____16. I enjoy making gourmet and/or high-calorie meals for others as long as I don't have to eat them myself.
a. Often   b. Sometimes   c. Rarely   d. Never

____17. The most powerful fear in my life is the fear of gaining weight or becoming fat.
a. Often   b. Sometimes   c. Rarely   d. Never

____18. I exercise a lot (more than 4 times per week and/or more than 4 hours per week) as a means of weight control.
a. True   b. False

____19. I find myself totally absorbed when reading books or magazines about dieting, exercising, and calorie counting to the point that I often spend hours studying them.
a. Often   b. Sometimes   c. Rarely   d. Never

____20. I tend to be a perfectionist and am not satisfied with myself unless I do things perfectly.
a. Almost always   b. Sometimes   c. Rarely   d. Never

____21. I go through long periods of time without eating (fasting) or eating very little as a means of weight control.
a. Often   b. Sometimes   c. Rarely   d. Never

____22. It is important to me to try to be thinner than all my friends.
a. Almost always   b. Sometimes   c. Rarely   d. Never

Bulimia Test (BT)

Chapter Link

This test is to be used with the Eating Disorders chapter of *Helping the Struggling Adolescent*.

Rapid Assessment Description

This questionnaire is designed to assess the symptoms of bulimia nervosa. It identifies behaviors related to extreme attempts to lose weight and provides criteria for ruling out anorexia nervosa.

Scoring Procedure

Response *e* on items 1–2, 6, 10, 16, 19, 22–23, 30 and response *a* on items 3–5, 8–9, 11–15, 17–18, 20–21, 24–29, 31–32, 35 are the most symptomatic of bulimic behavior. If your respondent circled this choice, the item is scored as a *5;* all adjacent alternatives are scored *4, 3, 2,* and *1* sequentially.

Total scores are the sum of all items except for items 7, 33–34, and 36, which are not included in the analysis; they are simply buffer items. Scores range from 32 to 160, with higher scores reflecting more serious bulimic symptoms.

The following items are used for subscales: *binges,* 1–4, 8, 11–12, 17–18, 22, 24, 28, 31, 35; *vomiting,* 1, 8, 15, 27, 30.

Permission

Available from the American Psychological Association, 1200 17th Street, N.W., Washington, DC 20036.

BT

Answer each question by circling the appropriate letter. Please respond to each item as honestly as possible; remember, all the information you provide will be kept strictly confidential.

1. Do you ever eat uncontrollably to the point of stuffing yourself (i.e., going on eating binges)?
   a. Once a month or less (never)
   b. 2–3 times a month
   c. Once or twice a week
   d. 3–6 times a day
   e. Once a day or more

2. I am satisfied with my eating patterns.
   a. Agree
   b. Neutral
   c. Disagree a little
   d. Disagree strongly

3. Have you ever kept eating until you thought you would explode?
   a. Practically every time I eat
   b. Very frequently
   c. Often
   d. Sometimes
   e. Seldom or never

4. Would you presently call yourself a "binge eater"?
   a. Yes, absolutely
   b. Yes
   c. Yes, probably
   d. Yes, possibly
   e. No, probably not

5. I prefer to eat
   a. At home alone
   b. At home with others
   c. In a public restaurant
   d. At a friend's house
   e. Doesn't matter

6. Do you feel you have control over the amount of food you consume?
   a. Most or all of the time
   b. A lot of the time
   c. Occasionally
   d. Rarely
   e. Never

7. I use laxatives or suppositories to help control my weight.
   a. Once a day or more
   b. 3–6 times a week
   c. Once or twice a week
   d. 2–3 times a month
   e. Once a month or less (or never)

8. I eat until I feel too tired to continue.
   a. At least once a day
   b. 3–6 times a week
   c. Once or twice a week
   d. 2–3 times a month
   e. Once a month or less (or never)

9. How often do you prefer eating ice cream, milkshakes, or pudding during a binge?
   a. Always
   b. Frequently
   c. Sometimes
   d. Seldom or never
   e. I don't binge

10. How much are you concerned about your eating binges?
    a. I don't binge
    b. Bothers me a little
    c. Moderate concern
    d. Major concern
    e. Probably the biggest concern in my life

11. Most people I know would be amazed if they knew how much food I can consume at one sitting.
    a. Without a doubt
    b. Very probably
    c. Probably
    d. Possibly
    e. No

12. Do you ever eat to the point of feeling sick?
    a. Very frequently
    b. Frequently
    c. Fairly often
    d. Occasionally
    e. Rarely or never

13. I am afraid to eat anything for fear that I won't be able to stop.
    a. Always
    b. Almost always
    c. Frequently
    d. Sometimes
    e. Seldom or never

14. I don't like myself after I eat too much.
    a. Always
    b. Frequently
    c. Sometimes
    d. Seldom or never
    e. I don't eat too much

15. How often do you intentionally vomit after eating?
    a. 2 or more times a week
    b. Once a week

c. 2–3 times a month
d. Once a month
e. Less than once a month (or never)

16. Which of the following describes your feelings after binge eating?
    a. I don't binge eat
    b. I feel O.K.
    c. I feel mildly upset with myself
    d. I feel quite upset with myself
    e. I hate myself

17. I eat a lot of food when I am not even hungry.
    a. Very frequently
    b. Frequently
    c. Occasionally
    d. Sometimes
    e. Seldom or never

18. My eating patterns are different from the eating patterns of most people.
    a. Always
    b. Almost always
    c. Frequently
    d. Sometimes
    e. Seldom or never

19. I have tried to lose weight by fasting or going on "crash" diets.
    a. Not in the past year
    b. Once in the past year
    c. 2–3 times in the past year
    d. 4–5 times in the past year
    e. More than 5 times in the past year

20. I feel sad or blue after eating more than I had planned to eat.
    a. Always
    b. Almost always
    c. Frequently
    d. Sometimes
    e. Seldom, never, or not applicable

21. When engaged in an eating binge, I tend to eat foods that are high in carbohydrates (sweets and starches).
    a. Always
    b. Almost always
    c. Frequently
    d. Sometimes
    e. Seldom, or I don't binge

22. Compared with most people, my ability to control my eating behavior seems to be
    a. Greater than others' ability
    b. About the same
    c. Less
    d. Much less
    e. I have absolutely no control

23. One of your best friends suddenly suggests that you both eat at a new restaurant buffet that night. Although you had planned on eating something light at home, you go ahead and eat out, eating quite a lot and feeling uncomfortably full. How would you feel about yourself on the ride home?
    a. Fine, glad I had tried that new restaurant
    b. A little regretful that I had eaten so much
    c. Somewhat disappointed in myself
    d. Upset with myself
    e. Totally disgusted with myself

24. I would presently label myself a "compulsive eater" (one who engages in episodes of uncontrolled eating).
    a. Absolutely
    b. Yes
    c. Yes, probably
    d. Yes, possibly
    e. No, probably not

25. What is the most weight you have ever lost in one month?
    a. Over 20 pounds
    b. 12–20 pounds
    c. 8–11 pounds
    d. 4–7 pounds
    e. Less than 4 pounds

26. If I eat too much at night I feel depressed the next morning.
    a. Always
    b. Frequently
    c. Sometimes
    d. Seldom or never
    e. I don't eat too much at night

27. Do you believe that it is easier for you to vomit than it is for most people?
    a. Yes, it's no problem at all for me
    b. Yes, it's easier
    c. Yes, it's a little easier
    d. About the same
    e. No, it's less easy

28. I feel that food controls my life.
    a. Always
    b. Almost always
    c. Frequently
    d. Sometimes
    e. Seldom or never

29. I feel depressed immediately after I eat too much.
    a. Always
    b. Frequently
    c. Sometimes
    d. Seldom or never
    e. I don't eat too much

30. How often do you vomit after eating in order to lose weight?
    a. Less than once a month (or never)
    b. Once a month
    c. 2–3 times a month
    d. Once a week
    e. 2 or more times a week

31. When consuming a large quantity of food, at what rate of speed do you usually eat?
    a. More rapidly than most people have ever eaten in their lives
    b. A lot more rapidly than most people
    c. A little more rapidly than most people
    d. About the same rate as most people
    e. More slowly than most people (or not applicable)

32. What is the most weight you have ever gained in one month?
    a. Over 20 pounds
    b. 12–20 pounds
    c. 8–11 pounds
    d. 4–7 pounds
    e. Less than 4 pounds

33. (Females only) My last menstrual period was
    a. Within the past month
    b. Within the past 2 months
    c. Within the past 4 months
    d. Within the past 6 months
    e. Not within the past 6 months

34. I use diuretics (water pills) to help control my weight.
    a. Once a day or more
    b. 3–6 times a week
    c. Once or twice a week
    d. 2–3 times a month
    e. Once a month or less (or never)

35. How do you think your appetite compares with that of most people you know?
    a. Many times larger than most
    b. Much larger
    c. A little larger
    d. About the same
    e. Smaller than most

36. (Females only) My menstrual cycles occur once a month.
    a. Always
    b. Usually
    c. Sometimes
    d. Seldom
    e. Never

Checklist for Making a Major Decision (CMMD)

Chapter Link

This checklist is to be used with the Decision Making chapter of *Helping the Struggling Adolescent*.

Rapid Assessment Description

This questionnaire presents a series of steps leading to discerning God's will on a particular matter. The checklist can help alert young people to factors that may need to be dealt with before God's will is revealed to them.

Scoring Procedure

The checklist is not to be tabulated or scored. It is simply a tool that clarifies the issues and delineates where a young person may be stuck in the process of discovering God's guidance.

Permission

The CMMD is adapted from *The Will of the Shepherd* by Dwight Carlson, M.D. Copyright © 1989 by Harvest House Publishers, Eugene, OR 97402. Used by permission.

Available from Dr. Dwight L. Carlson, 3250 Lomita Blvd., Suite 202, Torrance, CA 90505.

CMMD

Please complete the following questionnaire. It is arranged in a series of steps that help to reveal God's will. Answer the questions as honestly as possible.

The matter you want to know God's will about is _____

_____

Step 1: Be obedient to His already revealed will
  a. Have you accepted Jesus Christ as your personal Savior?   Yes   No
  b. Is there any known sin in your life?   Yes   No
  c. Are you being obedient to God's will to the extent to which it is now revealed?   Yes   No

Step 2: Be open to any means or results
  a. Are you willing to follow God's will when He reveals it to you, regardless of what His will is or what it might cost you?   Yes   No
  b. Are you open to any means He might choose to lead you, whether supernatural-miraculous or some less dramatic means?   Yes   No

Step 3: God's Word
  a. Do you have an adequate intake of God's Word?   Yes   No
  b. Are you familiar with what the Scriptures really say about the issue for which you are seeking guidance?   Yes   No

Step 4: Prayer
  a. Do you have a daily prayer time when you seek God's will and fellowship with Him?   Yes   No
  b. Have you specifically asked God's will regarding the matter for which you are seeking His guidance?   Yes   No
  c. Are you too busy to adequately meditate and wait on Him?   Yes   No

Step 5: The Holy Spirit
  a. Have you acknowledged the presence and function of the Holy Spirit in your life?   Yes   No
  b. Does the Holy Spirit now fill your life?   Yes   No

Step 6: Counsel
  a. Do you consistently fellowship with other Christians and hear God's Word proclaimed?   Yes   No
  b. Is there any possibility of a medical problem for which you should obtain help?   Yes   No
  c. Should you specifically seek the counsel of another, whether a minister, Christian friend, professional counselor, or someone else?   Yes   No

Step 7: Providential circumstances
  a. Have you adequately considered the providential circumstances that are available to you?   Yes   No

Step 8: Evaluation

a. Are you tired?   Yes   No

b. Have you specifically evaluated (preferably on paper) your underlying motives and the reasons for and against the decision you are considering?   Yes   No

c. Have you considered the needs of the world around you?   Yes   No

d. Have you considered your abilities?   Yes   No

e. Have you considered your desires and whether or not they are possible within God's will?   Yes   No

f. Will your decision harm your body or hurt others?   Yes   No

g. Will it hinder your spiritual growth, walk with Christ, or testimony?   Yes   No

h. Will it hinder the spiritual growth of others?   Yes   No

i. Is it the choice that is most pleasing to God?   Yes   No

j. Is it the best and wisest choice based on your enlightened judgment?   Yes   No

k. Have you prayerfully evaluated the matter alone, without unnecessary time pressure?   Yes   No

Step 9: The decision

a. Should you postpone the decision as to what God's will is in the matter?   Yes   No

b. Should you decide, but wait for its fulfillment?   Yes   No

c. Do you already know God's will but not His timing?   Yes   No

Step 10: God's peace

a. Having determined God's will in the matter, do you have a deep, inward peace about the decision?   Yes   No

b. As time passes and you continue to reflect and pray about the decision, do you have an increasing assurance from Him that the decision was the right one?   Yes   No

Child's Attitude Toward Father (CATF)

Chapter Link

This scale is to be used in conjunction with the Parents chapter of *Helping the Struggling Adolescent*.

Rapid Assessment Description

This questionnaire is designed to measure the extent, degree, or severity of problems a child has with his or her father.

Scoring Procedure

This scale is scored by first reverse-scoring items 2, 3, 8, 12, 14, 15, 16, 21, and 24. Next, total these scores and the scores of the other items, then subtract 25. This gives a range of scores from 0 to 100, with higher scores giving more evidence of the presence of problems with parents.

Permission

The CATF is copyright © 1982 by the Dorsey Press, Belmont, California. Reprinted by permission.

Available from the Dorsey Press, 224 South Michigan Avenue, Suite 440, Chicago, IL 60604.

CATF

This questionnaire is designed to measure the degree of contentment you have in your relationship with your father. It is not a test, so there are no right or wrong answers. Answer each item as carefully and accurately as you can by placing a number beside each one as follows:

1 = Rarely or none of the time
2 = A little of the time
3 = Some of the time
4 = A good part of the time
5 = Most or all of the time

_____ 1. My father gets on my nerves.

_____ 2. I get along well with my father.

_____ 3. I feel that I can really trust my father.

_____ 4. I dislike my father.

_____ 5. My father's behavior embarrasses me.

_____ 6. My father is too demanding.

_____ 7. I wish I had a different father.

_____ 8. I really enjoy my father.

_____ 9. My father puts too many limits on me.

_____10. My father interferes with my activities.

_____11. I resent my father.

_____12. I think my father is terrific.

_____13. I hate my father.

_____14. My father is very patient with me.

_____15. I really like my father.

_____16. I like being with my father.

_____17. I feel like I do not love my father.

_____18. My father is very irritating.

_____19. I feel very angry toward my father.

_____20. I feel violent toward my father.

_____21. I feel proud of my father.

_____22. I wish my father was more like others I know.

_____23. My father does not understand me.

_____24. I can really depend on my father.

_____25. I feel ashamed of my father.

Child's Attitude Toward Mother (CATM)

Chapter Link

This scale is to be used in conjunction with the Parents chapter of *Helping the Struggling Adolescent*.

Rapid Assessment Description

This questionnaire is designed to measure the extent, degree, or severity of problems a child has with his or her mother.

Scoring Procedure

This scale is scored by first reverse-scoring items 2, 3, 8, 12, 14, 15, 16, 21, and 24. Next, total these scores and the scores of the other items, then subtract 25. This gives a range of scores from 0 to 100, with higher scores giving more evidence of the presence of problems with parents.

Permission

The CATM is copyright © 1982 by the Dorsey Press. Reprinted by permission.

Available from the Dorsey Press, 224 South Michigan Avenue, Suite 440, Chicago, IL 60604.

CATM

This questionnaire is designed to measure the degree of contentment you have in your relationship with your mother. It is not a test, so there are no right or wrong answers. Answer each item as carefully and accurately as you can by placing a number beside each one as follows:

1 = Rarely or none of the time
2 = A little of the time
3 = Some of the time
4 = A good part of the time
5 = Most or all of the time

____ 1. My mother gets on my nerves.

____ 2. I get along well with my mother.

____ 3. I feel that I can really trust my mother.

____ 4. I dislike my mother.

____ 5. My mother's behavior embarrasses me.

____ 6. My mother is too demanding.

____ 7. I wish I had a different mother.

____ 8. I really enjoy my mother.

____ 9. My mother puts too many limits on me.

____10. My mother interferes with my activities.

____11. I resent my mother.

____12. I think my mother is terrific.

____13. I hate my mother.

____14. My mother is very patient with me.

____15. I really like my mother.

____16. I like being with my mother.

____17. I feel like I do not love my mother.

____18. My mother is very irritating.

____19. I feel very angry toward my mother.

____20. I feel violent toward my mother.

____21. I feel proud of my mother.

____22. I wish my mother was more like others I know.

____23. My mother does not understand me.

____24. I can really depend on my mother.

____25. I feel ashamed of my mother.

Clinical Anxiety Scale (CAS)

Chapter Link

This scale is to be used in conjunction with the Anxiety chapter of *Helping the Struggling Adolescent*.

Rapid Assessment Description

This questionnaire is designed to measure the amount of anxiety reported by the respondent. It is based on the clinical criteria for anxiety from the American Psychiatric Association's *Diagnostic and Statistical Manual, Third Edition, Revised* (DSM–III–R).

Scoring Procedure

The CAS is scored by first reverse-scoring items 1, 6, 7, 9, 13, 15, 16, and 17, totaling these and the scores of the other items, and subtracting 25. This gives a potential range of scores from 0 to 100. Higher scores indicate more severe anxiety.

Permission

The CAS is reprinted with permission from Walmyr Publishing Co., P.O. Box 24779, Tempe, AZ 85285. Copyright © 1984.

Available from Dr. Bruce A. Thyer, University of Georgia, School of Social Work, Athens, GA 30602.

CAS

This questionnaire is designed to measure how much anxiety you are currently feeling. It is not a test, so there are no right or wrong answers. Answer each item as carefully and as accurately as you can by placing a number beside each one as follows:

    1 = Rarely or none of the time
    2 = A little of the time
    3 = Some of the time
    4 = A good part of the time
    5 = Most or all of the time

_____ 1. I feel calm.

_____ 2. I feel tense.

_____ 3. I feel suddenly scared for no reason.

_____ 4. I feel nervous.

_____ 5. I use tranquilizers or antidepressants to cope with my anxiety.

_____ 6. I feel confident about the future.

_____ 7. I am free from senseless or unpleasant thoughts.

_____ 8. I feel afraid to go out of my house alone.

_____ 9. I feel relaxed and in control of myself.

_____10. I have spells of terror or panic.

_____11. I feel afraid in open spaces or in the streets.

_____12. I feel afraid I will faint in public.

_____13. I am comfortable traveling on buses, subways, or trains.

_____14. I feel nervousness or shakiness inside.

_____15. I feel comfortable in crowds, such as shopping or at a movie.

_____16. I feel comfortable when I am left alone.

_____17. I rarely feel afraid without good reason.

_____18. Due to my fears, I unreasonably avoid certain animals, objects, or situations.

_____19. I get upset easily or feel panicky unexpectedly.

_____20. My hands, arms or legs shake or tremble.

_____21. Due to my fears, I avoid social situations, whenever possible.

_____22. I experience sudden attacks of panic which catch me by surprise.

_____23. I feel generally anxious.

_____24. I am bothered by dizzy spells.

_____25. Due to my fears, I avoid being alone, whenever possible.

Cognitive Slippage Scale (CSS)

Chapter Link

This scale is to be used in conjunction with the Schizophrenia chapter of *Helping the Struggling Adolescent.*

Rapid Assessment Description

This scale is designed to measure cognitive slippages, an aspect of cognitive distortion that is viewed as a primary characteristic of schizophrenia. The CSS focuses mainly on speech deficits and confused thinking. Although the scale was developed to identify schizotypic characteristics, it may also be useful in identifying cognitive disorders among non-schizophrenics.

Scoring Procedure

The CSS is scored by assigning a score of 1 to the correct responses and then summing these scores. The correct response is "true" on items 2, 3, 4, 5, 9, 11, 13, 15, 18, 20, 22, 24, 25, 27, 28, 30, 31, 33. The remaining items are correct if answered "false."

Permission

Reprinted with permission from Michael L. Raulin.

Available from Dr. Michael L. Raulin, SUNY-Buffalo, Department of Psychology, Julian Park Hall, Buffalo, NY 14260.

CSS

Please circle either T *for True or* F *for False for each item as it applies to you.*

T   F   1. My thoughts are orderly most of the time.

T   F   2. I almost always feel as though my thoughts are on a different wavelength from 98% of the population.

T   F   3. Often when I am talking I feel that I am not making any sense.

T   F   4. Often people ask me a question and I don't know what it is that they are asking.

T   F   5. Often I don't even know what it is that I have just said.

T   F   6. I hardly ever find myself saying the opposite of what I meant to say.

T   F   7. I rarely feel so mixed up that I have difficulty functioning.

T   F   8. My thoughts are usually clear, at least to me.

T   F   9. My thoughts are more random than orderly.

T   F   10. The way I perceive things is much the same way in which others perceive them.

T   F   11. Sometimes my thoughts just disappear.

T   F   12. I can usually keep my thoughts going straight.

T   F   13. My thoughts are so vague and hazy that I wish I could just reach up and pull them into place.

T   F   14. I usually feel that people understand what I say.

T   F   15. There have been times when I have gone an entire day or longer without speaking.

T   F   16. I ordinarily don't get confused about *when* things happened.

T   F   17. It's usually easy to keep the point that I am trying to make clear in my mind.

T   F   18. My thoughts speed by so fast that I can't catch them.

T   F   19. I usually don't feel that I'm rambling on pointlessly when I'm speaking.

T   F   20. Sometimes when I try to focus on an idea, so many other thoughts come to mind that I find it impossible to concentrate on just one.

T   F   21. I have no difficulty in controlling my thoughts.

T   F   22. My thinking often gets "cloudy" for no apparent reason.

T   F   23. I think that I am reasonably good at communicating my ideas to other people.

T   F   24. I often find myself saying something that comes out completely backwards.

T   F   25. My thoughts often jump from topic to topic without any logical connection.

T   F   26. I'm pretty good at keeping track of time.

T   F   27. Often during the day I feel as though I am being flooded by thoughts.

T   F   28. The way that I process information is very different from the way in which other people do.

T   F   29. I have no difficulty separating past from present.

T   F   30. I often find that people are puzzled by what I say.

T   F   31. My thoughts seem to come and go so quickly that I can't keep up with them.

T   F   32. I can usually think things through clearly.

T   F   33. I often feel confused when I try to explain my ideas.

T   F   34. Usually my thoughts aren't difficult to keep track of.

T   F   35. I have no difficulty in controlling my thoughts.

Compulsive Eating Scale (CES)

Chapter Link

This scale is to be used in conjunction with the Body Image chapter of *Helping the Struggling Adolescent*.

Rapid Assessment Description

This inventory is designed to measure compulsive behaviors. The scale focuses specifically on overconcern with eating decisions and behaviors.

Scoring Procedure

All items are rated on 5-point scales but have different categories for various items. The letters used in the rating scale are converted to numbers as follows: $a = 1, b = 2, c = 3, d = 4, e = 5$. Scores are the sum of the item ratings and range from 8 to 40. Higher scores indicate more compulsivity in one's eating.

Permission

Reprinted with permission from *Adolescence* 19:15–29, D. M. Kagan and R. L. Squires, "Eating Disorders Among Adolescents: Patterns and Prevalence," copyright © 1984 by Libra Publishers, Inc.

Available from Libra Publishers, Inc., 3089C Clairmont Drive, Suite 383, San Diego, CA 92117.

CES

How often do you do each of the following activities? Circle the one answer for each question that comes closest to describing you.

1. Eat because you are feeling lonely.
   a. Never
   b. Once or twice a year
   c. Once a month
   d. Once a week
   e. More than once a week

2. Feel completely out of control when it comes to food.
   a. Never
   b. Once or twice a year
   c. Once a month
   d. Once a week
   e. More than once a week

3. Eat so much that your stomach hurts.
   a. Never
   b. Once or twice a year
   c. Once a month
   d. Once a week
   e. More than once a week

4. Eat too much because you are upset or nervous.
   a. Never
   b. Once or twice a year
   c. Once a month
   d. Once a week
   e. More than once a week

5. Eat too much because you are bored.
   a. Never
   b. Once or twice a year
   c. Once a month
   d. Once a week
   e. More than once a week

6. Go out with friends just for the purpose of overstuffing yourself with food.
   a. Never
   b. Once or twice a year
   c. Once a month
   d. Once a week
   e. More than once a week

7. Eat so much food so fast that you don't know how much you ate or how it tasted.
   a. Never
   b. Once or twice a year
   c. Once a month
   d. Once a week
   e. More than once a week

8. Get out of bed at night, go into the kitchen, and finish the remains of some delicious food because you knew it was there.
   a. Never
   b. Once or twice a year
   c. Once a month
   d. Once a week
   e. More than once a week

Compulsiveness Inventory (CI)

Chapter Link

This inventory is to be used in conjunction with the Obsessions and Compulsions chapter of *Helping the Struggling Adolescent.*

Rapid Assessment Description

This inventory is designed to measure compulsive behaviors that are common in the normal population. This scale focuses on overconcern with decisions and tasks to be completed perfectly. It measures three aspects of compulsivity: indecision and double-checking (IDC), order and regularity (OR), detail and perfection (DP). The total score on the CI can also be used as a general measure of compulsiveness.

Scoring Procedure

The scores on the CI are the total number of *Yes* responses. Items for the subscales are as follows: IDC, 1–5; DP, 6–9; OR, 10–11. Higher scores indicate more compulsive behavior.

Permission

Reprinted with permission from *Psychological Reports* 57:559–63, D. M. Kagan and R. L. Squires, "Measuring Non-pathological Compulsiveness," copyright © 1985 by Libra Publishers, Inc.

Available from Libra Publishers, Inc., 3089C Clairmont Drive, Suite 383, San Diego, CA 92117.

CI

Respond to each question below by circling Yes *or* No.

Yes   No   1. Do you have time to turn things over and over in your mind for a long time before being able to decide what to do?

Yes   No   2. Do you often have to check things several times?

Yes   No   3. Do you ever have to do things over again a certain number of times before they seem quite right?

Yes   No   4. Do you have difficulty making up your mind?

Yes   No   5. Do you have to go back and check doors, cupboards, or windows to make sure they are really shut?

Yes   No   6. Do you dislike having a room untidy or not quite clean for a short time?

Yes   No   7. Do you take great care in hanging and folding your clothes at night?

Yes   No   8. Do you like to keep a certain order to undressing and dressing or washing or bathing?

Yes   No   9. Do you like to put your personal belongings in set places?

Yes   No   10. Do you like to get things done exactly right down to the smallest detail?

Yes   No   11. Are you the sort of person who has to pay a great deal of attention to details?

Concern Over Weight and Dieting Scale (COWD)

Chapter Link

This scale is to be used in conjunction with the Eating Disorders chapter of *Helping the Struggling Adolescent*.

Rapid Assessment Description

This scale is designed to measure concerns over weight and dieting as symptoms of eating disorders in high school students.

Scoring Procedure

All items are rated on 5-point scales, although there are different response categories for various items. The letters used in rating responses are converted to the following numeric values: $a = 1, b = 2, c = 3, d = 4, e = 5$. Scores are the sum of all item responses and range from 14 to 70. Higher scores indicate greater concern over one's weight and diet.

Permission

Reprinted with permission from *Adolescence* 19:15–29, D. M. Kagan and R. L. Squires, "Eating Disorders Among Adolescents: Patterns and Prevalence," copyright © 1984 by Libra Publishers, Inc.

Available from Libra Publishers, Inc., 3089C Clairmont Drive, Suite 383, San Diego, CA 92117.

COWD

For the following questions please answer each by circling the alternative that is most true for you.

1. The worst thing about being fat is
   a. No opinion
   b. Getting teased
   c. Feeling unsexy
   d. Being unpopular
   e. Feeling bad about yourself

2. What is the greatest amount of weight you ever lost on a diet?
   a. Never on a diet
   b. 10 lbs
   c. 11–19 lbs
   d. 20–29 lbs
   e. 30 lbs or more

3. Do you think you are overweight now?
   a. Don't know
   b. No
   c. Yes, by less than 10 lbs
   d. Yes: 10–19 lbs
   e. Yes: by 20 lbs or more

4. How often do you skip one meal so you will lose weight?
   a. Never
   b. Once or twice a year
   c. Once a month
   d. Once a week
   e. More than once a week

5. How often do you avoid eating fattening foods like candy so you will lose weight?
   a. Never
   b. Once or twice a year
   c. Once a month
   d. Once a week
   e. More than once a week

6. How often do you hate yourself or feel guilty because you cannot stop overeating?
   a. Never
   b. Once or twice a year
   c. Once a month
   d. Once a week
   e. More than once a week

7. How often do you go without eating solid food for 24 hours or more so you will lose weight?
   a. Never
   b. Once or twice a year
   c. Once a month
   d. Once a week
   e. More than once a week

8. If a special weight-control course were offered at this school, would you take it?
   a. No opinion
   b. No
   c. Probably no
   d. Probably yes
   e. Definitely yes

9. How often do you feel guilty after eating?
   a. Never
   b. Once in a while
   c. Frequently
   d. Very frequently
   e. All the time

10. How often are you aware of the calorie content of the food you eat?
    a. Never
    b. Once in a while
    c. Frequently
    d. Very frequently
    e. All the time

11. How old were you when you first started worrying about your weight?
    a. Never
    b. 12 years or less
    c. 13–14 years
    d. 15–16 years
    e. 17–18 years

How many times have you tried each of the weight-loss methods listed below?

12. Diet medicine (pills, liquids, or powders)
    a. Never
    b. Once
    c. Twice
    d. Three times
    e. More than three times

13. Health spa or exercise class (including aerobic dancing)
    a. Never
    b. Once
    c. Twice
    d. Three times
    e. More than three times

14. Diet published in a book or magazine or recommended by a friend or relative
    a. Never
    b. Once
    c. Twice
    d. Three times
    e. More than three times

Dysfunctional Attitude Scale (DAS)

Chapter Link

This scale is to be used in conjunction with the Depression chapter of *Helping the Struggling Adolescent*.

Rapid Assessment Description

This questionnaire is designed to identify cognitive distortions, particularly the distortions that may underlie or cause depression. The items on the DAS are constructed so as to represent seven major value systems: approval, love, achievement, perfectionism, entitlement, omnipotence, and autonomy.

Scoring Procedure

The DAS is easily scored by using zeros for items omitted, assigning a score of 1 (on a 7-point scale) to the adaptive end of the scale, and simply summing up the scores on all items. With no items omitted, scores on the DAS range from 40 to 280, with lower scores equaling more adaptive beliefs (fewer cognitive distortions).

Permission

Reprinted with permission from Arlene N. Weissman, Ph.D.

Available from Dr. Arlene Weissman, 1500 Market Street, Philadelphia, PA 19102.

DAS

For each of the attitudes, indicate to the left of the item the number that best describes how you think. Be sure to choose only one answer for each attitude. Because people are different, there are no right or wrong answers to these statements. To decide whether a given attitude is typical of your way of looking at things, simply keep in mind what you are like most of the time.

> 1 = Totally agree
> 2 = Agree very much
> 3 = Agree slightly
> 4 = Neutral
> 5 = Disagree slightly
> 6 = Disagree very much
> 7 = Totally disagree

_____ 1. It is difficult to be happy unless one is good-looking, intelligent, rich, and creative.

_____ 2. Happiness is more a matter of my attitude towards myself than the way other people feel about me.

_____ 3. People will probably think less of me if I make a mistake.

_____ 4. If I do not do well all the time, people will not respect me.

_____ 5. Taking even a small risk is foolish because the loss is likely to be a disaster.

_____ 6. It is possible to gain another person's respect without being especially talented at anything.

_____ 7. I cannot be happy unless most people I know admire me.

_____ 8. If a person asks for help, it is a sign of weakness.

_____ 9. If I do not do as well as other people, it means I am a weak person.

_____10. If I fail at my work, then I am a failure as a person.

_____11. If you cannot do something well, there is little point in doing it at all.

_____12. Making mistakes is fine because I can learn from them.

_____13. If someone disagrees with me, it probably indicates he does not like me.

_____14. If I fail partly, it is as bad as being a complete failure.

_____15. If other people know what you are really like, they will think less of you.

_____16. I am nothing if a person I love doesn't love me.

_____17. One can get pleasure from an activity regardless of the end result.

_____18. People should have a chance to succeed before doing anything.

_____19. My value as a person depends greatly on what others think of me.

_____20. If I don't set the highest standards for myself, I am likely to end up a second-rate person.

_____21. If I am to be a worthwhile person, I must be the best in at least one way.

_____22. People who have good ideas are better than those who do not.

_____23. I should be upset if I make a mistake.

_____24. My own opinions of myself are more important than others' opinions of me.

_____25. To be a good, moral, worthwhile person I must help everyone who needs it.

_____26. If I ask a question, it makes me look stupid.

_____27. It is awful to be put down by people important to you.

_____28. If you don't have other people to lean on, you are going to be sad.

_____29. I can reach important goals without pushing myself.

_____30. It is possible for a person to be scolded and not get upset.

_____31. I cannot trust other people because they might be cruel to me.

_____32. If others dislike you, you cannot be happy.

_____33. It is best to give up your own interests in order to please other people.

_____34. My happiness depends more on other people than it does on me.

_____35. I do not need the approval of other people in order to be happy.

_____36. If a person avoids problems, the problems tend to go away.

_____37. I can be happy even if I miss out on many of the good things in life.

_____38. What other people think of me is very important.

_____39. Being alone leads to unhappiness.

_____40. I can find happiness without being loved by another person.

Eating Attitudes Test (EAT)

Chapter Link

This test is to be used in conjunction with the Eating Disorders chapter of *Helping the Struggling Adolescent.*

Rapid Assessment Description

This test is designed to measure a broad range of behaviors and attitudes that characterize anorexia nervosa. This instrument is helpful in identifying young people with serious eating concerns even if they do not show the weight loss that is characteristic of anorexia nervosa.

Scoring Procedure

The forty items are scored in terms of how frequently the person experiences them. Items 1, 18, 19, 23, and 39 are scored as follows: $6 = 3; 5 = 2; 4 = 1;$ and $3, 2,$ and $1 = 0$. The remaining items are scored as follows: $1 = 2; 2 = 2; 3 = 1;$ and $4, 5,$ and $6 = 0$. Items 2–17, 20, 21, 22, 24, 25, 26, 28–38, and 40 when marked *Always* and items 1, 18, 19, 23, and 39 when marked *Never* indicate anorexia. Total scores are the sum of the item values; they range from 0 to 120.

Permission

Reprinted with permission from David M. Garner, Ph.D.

Available from Dr. David M. Garner, Department of Psychiatry, West Free Hall, Michigan State University, East Lansing, MI 48824-1316.

EAT

Please indicate on the line at the left the answer that applies best to each of the numbered statements. All of the results will be strictly confidential. Most of the questions directly relate to food or eating, although other types of questions have been included. Please answer each question carefully.

1 = Always
2 = Very often
3 = Often
4 = Sometimes
5 = Rarely
6 = Never

_____ 1. Like eating with other people.

_____ 2. Prepare foods for others but do not eat what I cook.

_____ 3. Become anxious prior to eating.

_____ 4. Am terrified about being overweight.

_____ 5. Avoid eating when I am hungry.

_____ 6. Find myself preoccupied with food.

_____ 7. Have gone on eating binges where I feel that I may not be able to stop.

_____ 8. Cut my food into small pieces.

_____ 9. Aware of the calorie content of foods that I eat.

_____10. Particularly avoid food with a high carbohydrate content (e.g., bread, potatoes, rice, etc.).

_____11. Feel bloated after meals.

_____12. Feel that others would prefer if I ate more.

_____13. Vomit after I have eaten.

_____14. Feel extremely guilty after eating.

_____15. Am preoccupied with a desire to be thinner.

_____16. Exercise strenuously to burn off calories.

_____17. Weigh myself several times a day.

_____18. Like my clothes to fit tightly.

_____19. Enjoy eating meat.

_____20. Wake up early in the morning.

_____21. Eat the same foods day after day.

_____22. Think about burning my calories when I exercise.

_____23. Have regular menstrual periods.

_____24. Other people think that I am too thin.

_____25. Am preoccupied with the thought of having fat on my body.

_____26. Take longer than others to eat my meals.

_____27. Enjoy eating at restaurants.

_____28. Take laxatives.

_____29. Avoid foods with sugar in them.

_____30. Eat diet foods.

_____31. Feel that food controls my life.

_____32. Display self-control around food.

_____33. Feel that others pressure me to eat.

_____34. Give too much time and thought to food.

_____35. Suffer from constipation.

_____36. Feel uncomfortable after eating sweets.

_____37. Engage in dieting behavior.

_____38. Like my stomach to be empty.

_____39. Enjoy trying new rich foods.

_____40. Have the impulse to vomit after meals.

Family Adaptability and Cohesion Evaluation Scale (FACES–III)

Chapter Link

This scale is to be used in conjunction with the Parents chapter of *Helping the Struggling Adolescent*.

Rapid Assessment Description

This scale is designed to measure two main dimensions of family functioning: cohesion and adaptability. It is the result of Dr. David H. Olson's research on the systematic assessment and treatment of families and is based on his Circumplex Model of family functioning, which asserts that there are three central dimensions of family behavior: cohesion, adaptability (ability to change), and communication. A full description of his work and the Circumplex Model can be found in the book *Circumplex Model* (Binghamton, NY: Haworth Press, 1989).

Scoring Procedure

FACES–III is scored by summing all items to obtain the total score, summing odd items to obtain the cohesion score, and summing even items to obtain the adaptability score. The higher the cohesion score, the more enmeshed the family is said to be. The higher the adaptability score, the more chaotic the family is said to be.

Permission

Reprinted with permission of David H. Olson, Ph.D.

Available from Dr. David H. Olson, Family Social Science, University of Minnesota, 290 McNeal Hall, 1985 Buford Avenue, St. Paul, MN 55108.

FACES–III

Please use the following scale to answer both sets of questions.

1 = Almost never
2 = Once in a while
3 = Sometimes
4 = Frequently
5 = Almost always

Describe your family now:

____ 1. Family members ask each other for help.

____ 2. In solving problems, the children's suggestions are followed.

____ 3. We approve of each other's friends.

____ 4. Children have a say in their discipline.

____ 5. We like to do things with just our immediate family.

____ 6. Different persons act as leaders in our family.

____ 7. Family members feel closer to other family members than to people outside of the family.

____ 8. Our family changes its way of handling tasks.

____ 9. Family members like to spend free time with each other.

____10. Parent(s) and children discuss punishment together.

____11. Family members feel very close to each other.

____12. The children make the decisions in our family.

____13. When our family gets together for activities, everybody is present.

____14. Rules change in our family.

____15. We can easily think of things to do together as a family.

____16. We shift household responsibilities from person to person.

____17. Family members consult other family members on their decisions.

____18. It is hard to identify the leader(s) in our family.

____19. Family togetherness is very important.

____20. It is hard to tell who does which household chores.

Ideally, how would you like your family to be:

____21. Family members would ask each other for help.

____22. In solving problems, the children's suggestions would be followed.

____23. We would approve of each other's friends.

____24. The children would have a say in their discipline.

____25. We would like to do things with just our immediate family.

____26. Different persons would act as leaders in our family.

____27. Family members would feel closer to each other than to people outside the family.

____28. Our family would change its way of handling tasks.

____29. Family members would like to spend free time with each other.

____30. Parent(s) and children would discuss punishment together.

____31. Family members would feel very close to each other.

____32. Children would make the decisions in our family.

____33. When our family got together, everybody would be present.

____34. Rules would change in our family.

____35. We could easily think of things to do together as a family.

____36. We would shift household responsibilities from person to person.

____37. Family members would consult each other on their decisions.

____38. We would know who the leader(s) was (were) in our family.

____39. Family togetherness would be very important.

____40. We could tell who does which household chores.

Fear Questionnaire (FQ)

Chapter Link

This questionnaire is to be used in conjunction with the Phobia chapter of *Helping the Struggling Adolescent.*

Rapid Assessment Description

This instrument assesses the outcome of work with phobic patients. The form is general enough to be useful with any phobic disorder, but has added precision because it allows the practitioner to specify the phobia that is the focus of treatment.

Scoring Procedure

All items are rated on a scale from 1 to 8, with higher scores reflecting more severe phobic responses. The total phobia rating is the sum of the scores for items 2 through 16. Scores range from 0 to 120.

Permission

Reprinted with permission from *Behavior Research and Therapy* 17:263–67, I. M. Marks and A. M. Matthews, "Brief Standard Self-rating for Phobic Patient," copyright © 1978.

Available from Journals Permissions, 395 Saw Mill River Road, Elmsford, NY 10523.

FQ

Choose a number from the scale below to show how much you would avoid each of the situations listed because of fear or other unpleasant feelings.

- 0   Would not avoid it
- 2   Would slightly avoid It
- 4   Would definitely avoid it
- 6   Would markedly avoid it
- 8   Would always avoid it

1. The main phobia you want treated (describe in your own words):

_____

_____

_____ 2. Injections or minor surgery

_____ 3. Eating or drinking with other people

_____ 4. Hospitals

_____ 5. Traveling alone by bus or coach

_____ 6. Walking alone in busy streets

_____ 7. Being watched or stared at

_____ 8. Going into crowded shops

_____ 9. Talking to people in authority

_____10. Sight of blood

_____11. Being criticized

_____12. Going alone far from home

_____13. Thought of injury or illness

_____14. Speaking or acting to an audience

_____15. Large open spaces

_____16. Going to the dentist

_____17. Other situations (describe) _____

_____

How would you rate the present state of your phobic symptoms on the scale below?

- 0   No phobias present
- 2   Slightly disturbing
- 4   Definitely disturbing
- 6   Markedly disturbing
- 8   Very severely disturbing/disabling

Fear Survey Schedule–II (FSS–II)

Chapter Link

This survey schedule is to be used in conjunction with the Phobia chapter of *Helping the Struggling Adolescent*.

Rapid Assessment Description

The FSS–II is designed to measure fear responses. The instrument lists potential fear-evoking situations and stimuli, and the young person rates his or her level of discomfort or stress.

Scoring Procedure

Each item is rated on a 7-point scale of intensity of fear. Scores are the sum of the item scores, and they range from 51 to 357. Higher scores indicate greater fear.

Permission

Reprinted with permission from *Behavior Research and Therapy* 3:45–53, J. H. Geer, "The Development of a Scale to Measure Fear," copyright © 1965 Pergamon Press, Inc.

Available from Journal Permissions, 395 Saw Mill River Road, Elmsford, NY 10523.

FSS–II

Listed below are fifty-one different stimuli that can cause fear in people. Please rate how much fear you feel about each by using the following rating scale.

1 = None
2 = Very little fear
3 = A little fear
4 = Some fear
5 = Much fear
6 = Very much fear
7 = Terror

_____ 1. Sharp objects

_____ 2. Being a passenger in a car

_____ 3. Dead bodies

_____ 4. Suffocating

_____ 5. Failing a test

_____ 6. Looking foolish

_____ 7. Being a passenger in an airplane

_____ 8. Worms

_____ 9. Arguing with parents

_____10. Rats and mice

_____11. Life after death

_____12. Hypodermic needles

_____13. Being criticized

_____14. Meeting someone for the first time

_____15. Roller coasters

_____16. Being alone

_____17. Making mistakes

_____18. Being misunderstood

_____19. Death

_____20. Being in a fight

_____21. Crowded places

_____22. Blood

_____23. Heights

_____24. Being a leader

_____25. Swimming alone

_____26. Illness

_____27. Being with drunks

_____28. Illness or injury to loved ones

_____29. Being self-conscious

_____30. Driving a car

_____31. Meeting authority

____32. Mental illness

____33. Closed places

____34. Boating

____35. Spiders

____36. Thunderstorms

____37. Not being a success

____38. God

____39. Snakes

____40. Cemeteries

____41. Speaking before a group

____42. Seeing a fight

____43. Death of a loved one

____44. Dark places

____45. Strange dogs

____46. Deep water

____47. Being with a member of the opposite sex

____48. Stinging insects

____49. Untimely or early death

____50. Losing a job

____51. Auto accidents

Generalized Contentment Scale (GCS)

Chapter Link

This scale is to be used in conjunction with the Depression and Suicide chapters of *Helping the Struggling Adolescent*.

Rapid Assessment Description

This questionnaire is designed to measure the degree, severity, or magnitude of nonpsychotic depression. The GCS focuses largely on affective aspects of clinical depression, examining respondents' feelings about a number of behaviors, attitudes, and events associated with depression.

Scoring Procedure

The GCS is scored by first reverse-scoring items 5, 8, 9, 11, 12, 13, 15, 16, 21, 22, 23, and 24 and totaling these and the other item scores, then subtracting 25. This gives a range of 0 to 100, with higher scores indicating more depression.

Permission

Reprinted with permission. Copyright © 1982 by the Dorsey Press.

Available from the Dorsey Press, 224 South Michigan Avenue, Suite 440, Chicago, IL 60604.

GCS

This questionnaire is designed to measure the degree of contentment that you feel about your life and surroundings. It is not a test, so there are no right or wrong answers. Answer each item as carefully and accurately as you can by placing a number beside each one as follows:

1 = Rarely or none of the time
2 = A little of the time
3 = Some of the time
4 = Good part of the time
5 = Most or all of the time

_____ 1. I feel powerless to do anything about my life.

_____ 2. I feel blue.

_____ 3. I am restless and can't keep still.

_____ 4. I have crying spells.

_____ 5. It is easy for me to relax.

_____ 6. I have a hard time getting started on things that I need to do.

_____ 7. I do not sleep well at night.

_____ 8. When things get tough, I feel there is always someone I can turn to.

_____ 9. I feel that the future looks bright for me.

_____10. I feel downhearted.

_____11. I feel that I am needed.

_____12. I feel that I am appreciated by others.

_____13. I enjoy being active and busy.

_____14. I feel that others would be better off without me.

_____15. I enjoy being with other people.

_____16. I feel it is easy for me to make decisions.

_____17. I feel downtrodden.

_____18. I am irritable.

_____19. I get upset easily.

_____20. I feel that I don't deserve to have a good time.

_____21. I have a full life.

_____22. I feel that people really care about me.

_____23. I have a great deal of fun.

_____24. I feel great in the morning.

_____25. I feel that my situation is hopeless.

Goldfarb Fear of Fat Scale (GFFS)

Chapter Link

This scale is to be used in conjunction with the Eating Disorder chapter of *Helping the Struggling Adolescent*.

Rapid Assessment Description

The GFFS measures one of the underlying emotional experiences of eating disorders, the fear of becoming fat. The test is useful in identifying young people at risk for bulimia or anorexia, and it is useful in assessing the state of those already suffering from these disorders.

Scoring Procedure

Each item is rated on a scale from 1 to 4, from *Very untrue* to *Very true*. Scores are the sum of all items. Scores range from 10 to 40, with high scores indicating more fear of gaining weight.

Permission

Reprinted with permission from *Journal of Personality Assessment* 49:329–32, L. A. Goldfarb, E. M. Dykens, and M. Gerrard, "The Goldfarb Fear of Fat Scale," copyright © 1985 by Lawrence Erlbaum Associates, Inc., Publishers.

Available from Lawrence Erlbaum Associates, Inc., 365 Broadway, Hillsdale, NJ 07642.

GFFS

Please read each of the following statements and select the number that best represents your feelings and beliefs.

        1 = Very untrue
        2 = Somewhat untrue
        3 = Somewhat true
        4 = Very true

___ 1. My biggest fear is of becoming fat.

___ 2. I am afraid to gain even a little weight.

___ 3. I believe there is a real risk that I will become overweight someday.

___ 4. I don't understand how overweight people can live with themselves.

___ 5. Becoming fat would be the worst thing that could happen to me.

___ 6. If I stopped concentrating on controlling my weight, chances are I would become very fat.

___ 7. There is nothing that I can do to make the thought of gaining weight less painful and frightening.

___ 8. I feel like all my energy goes into controlling my weight.

___ 9. If I eat even a little, I may lose control and not stop eating.

___10. Staying hungry is the only way I can guard against losing control and becoming fat.

Guilt Scale (GS)

Chapter Link

This scale is to be used in conjunction with the Guilt chapter of *Helping the Struggling Adolescent*.

Rapid Assessment Description

This scale is designed to indicate the degree to which an individual struggles with the emotion of guilt.

Scoring Procedure

This scale is scored by totaling the scores of all the items and subtracting 25. This provides a range of scores from 0 to 100, with a higher score indicating more guilt feelings. While this quick assessment is not empirically based, it can serve as a springboard to examining the intensity of a person's guilt feelings.

Permission

The scale has been devised by Les Parrott III and is available from Les Parrott, Department of Psychology, Seattle Pacific University, Seattle, WA 98109.

GS

The following questions are a way to assess your feelings of guilt. There are no right or wrong answers. Take as much time as you need. Answer each item as carefully and as accurately as you can by placing a number beside each of the items as follows:

1 = Rarely or none of the time
2 = A little of the time
3 = Some of the time
4 = Good part of the time
5 = Most or all of the time

_____ 1. I worry about what others think of me.

_____ 2. I believe I should always be generous.

_____ 3. I feel I should be punished.

_____ 4. I believe I am guilty.

_____ 5. I believe I should not be angry.

_____ 6. I take a hard look at myself.

_____ 7. I feel ashamed.

_____ 8. I punish myself.

_____ 9. I detest myself for my failures.

_____10. A guilty conscience bothers me.

_____11. I believe I should not lose my temper.

_____12. I feel guilty.

_____13. I am fretful.

_____14. When I feel guilty, it lasts a long time.

_____15. I feel I am unforgivable.

_____16. I feel I am a reject.

_____17. I detest myself for my thoughts.

_____18. I feel nervous about others' opinions of me.

_____19. I believe I should not hurt another person's feelings.

_____20. I fear something bad will happen to me in the future.

_____21. I have spells of very intense guilt.

_____22. I avoid some places due to my guilt feelings.

_____23. I cannot tell the difference between feeling guilty and being guilty.

_____24. I avoid some people due to my guilt feelings.

_____25. I avoid being alone because of my guilt feelings.

Hare Self-Esteem Scale (HSS)

Chapter Link

This scale is to be used in conjunction with the Inferiority chapter of *Helping the Struggling Adolescent*.

Rapid Assessment Description

This scale measures self-esteem of school-age children ten years old and above. The HSS consists of three ten-item subscales that are area-specific (peer, school, home). The sum of all thirty items is viewed as a general self-esteem measure. Items were chosen to include both self-evaluative and other evaluative items.

Scoring Procedure

After reverse-scoring negatively worded items, the items for the subscales are summed using the following scale: $a = 1$, $b = 2$, $c = 3$, $d = 4$. The three subscale scores are totaled to produce the score for the general self-esteem scale. Higher scores indicate higher self-esteem.

Permission

Reprinted with permission from Bruce R. Hare.

Available from Dr. Bruce R. Hare, SUNY–Stony Brook, Department of Sociology, Stony Brook, NY 11794-4356.

HSS

HSS–Peer

In the blank provided, please write the letter of the answer that best describes how you feel about the sentence. These sentences are designed to find out how you generally feel when you are with other people your age. There are no right or wrong answers.

> a = Strongly disagree
> b = Disagree
> c = Agree
> d = Strongly agree

____ 1. I have at least as many friends as other people my age.

____ 2. I am not as popular as other people my age.

____ 3. In the kinds of things that people my age like to do, I am at least as good as most other people.

____ 4. People my age often pick on me.

____ 5. Other people think I am a lot of fun to be with.

____ 6. I usually keep to myself because I am not like other people my age.

____ 7. Other people wish that they were like me.

____ 8. I wish I were a different kind of person because I would have more friends.

____ 9. If my group of friends decided to vote for leaders of their group, I'd be elected to a high position.

____10. When things get tough, I am not a person whom other people my age would turn to for help.

HSS–Home

In the blank provided, please write the letter of the answer that best describes how you feel about the sentence. These sentences are designed to find out how you generally feel when you are with your family. There are no right or wrong answers.

> a = Strongly disagree
> b = Disagree
> c = Agree
> d = Strongly agree

____ 1. My parents are proud of the kind of person I am.

____ 2. No one pays much attention to me at home.

____ 3. My parents feel that I can be depended on.

____ 4. I often feel that if they could, my parents would trade me in for another child.

____ 5. My parents try to understand me.

____ 6. My parents expect too much of me.

___ 7. I am an important person to my family.

___ 8. I often feel unwanted at home.

___ 9. My parents believe that I will be a success in the future.

___10. I often wish that I had been born into another family.

HSS–School

In the blank provided, please write the letter of the answer that best describes how you feel about the sentence. These sentences are designed to find out how you generally feel when you are in school. There are no right or wrong answers.

        a = Strongly disagree
        b = Disagree
        c = Agree
        d = Strongly agree

___ 1. My teachers expect too much of me.

___ 2. In the kinds of things we do in school, I am at least as good as other people in my classes.

___ 3. I often feel worthless in school.

___ 4. I am usually proud of my report card.

___ 5. School is harder for me than for most other people.

___ 6. My teachers are usually happy with the kind of work I do.

___ 7. Most of my teachers do not understand me.

___ 8. I am an important person in my classes.

___ 9. It seems that no matter how hard I try I never get the grades I deserve.

___10. All in all, I feel I've been very fortunate to have had the kinds of teachers I've had since I started school.

Index of Self-Esteem (ISE)

Chapter Link

This index is to be used in conjunction with the Inferiority chapter of *Helping the Struggling Adolescent*.

Rapid Assessment Description

This questionnaire is designed to measure the degree, severity, or magnitude of a problem with self-esteem. Because problems with self-esteem are often central to social and psychological difficulties, this instrument has a wide range of utility for a number of struggles.

Scoring Procedure

The ISE is scored by first reverse-scoring the following items: 3, 4, 5, 6, 7, 14, 15, 18, 21, 22, 23, 25. Next, total these and the other item scores and subtract 25. This gives a range of 1 to 100, with higher scores giving more evidence of the presence of problems with self-esteem. Scores above 30 indicate the possibility of a clinically significant problem; scores below 30 indicate the person probably has no such problem.

Permission

ISE

This questionnaire is designed to measure how you see yourself. It is not a test, so there are no right or wrong answers. Please answer each item as carefully and accurately as you can by placing a number by each item.

1 = Rarely or none of the time
2 = A little of the time
3 = Some of the time
4 = A good part of the time
5 = Most or all of the time

_____ 1. I feel that people would not like me if they really knew me well.

_____ 2. I feel that others get along much better than I do.

_____ 3. I feel that I am a beautiful person.

_____ 4. When I am with other people I feel they are glad I am with them.

_____ 5. I feel that people really like to talk with me.

_____ 6. I feel that I am a very competent person.

_____ 7. I think I make a good impression on others.

_____ 8. I feel that I need more self-confidence.

_____ 9. When I am with strangers I am very nervous.

_____10. I think that I am a dull person.

_____11. I feel ugly.

_____12. I feel that others have more fun than I do.

_____13. I feel that I bore people.

_____14. I think my friends find me interesting.

_____15. I think I have a good sense of humor.

_____16. I feel very self-conscious when I am with strangers.

_____17. I feel that if I could be more like other people I would "have it made."

_____18. I feel that people have a good time when they are with me.

_____19. I feel like a wallflower when I go out.

_____20. I feel I get pushed around more than others.

_____21. I think I am a rather nice person.

_____22. I feel that people really like me very much.

_____23. I feel that I am a likable person.

_____24. I am afraid I will appear foolish to others.

_____25. My friends think very highly of me.

Intense Ambivalence Scale (IAS)

Chapter Link

This scale is to be used in conjunction with the Schizophrenia chapter of *Helping the Struggling Adolescent*.

Rapid Assessment Description

This scale is designed to measure intense ambivalence, which is the existence of simultaneous or rapidly interchangeable positive and negative feelings toward the same object or activity, with both positive and negative feelings being strong.

Scoring Procedure

The IAS is scored by assigning a score of 1 to the correct responses and then summing them. The correct response is *True* on items 1, 4, 5, 7–22, 24, 26, 27, 30, 31, 32, 34, 35, 37, 38, 40, 42, 43, and 45 and *False* for the remainder of the items.

Permission

Reprinted with permission from *Journal of Consulting and Clinical Psychology* 52:63–72, Michael L. Raulin, "Development of a Scale to Measure Intense Ambivalence," copyright © 1984 by the American Psychological Association.

Available from Dr. Michael L. Raulin, SUNY–Buffalo, Department of Psychology, Julian Park Hall, Buffalo, NY 14260.

IAS

Circle either T *for True or* F *for False for each item as it applies to you.*

T   F   1. Very often, even my favorite pastimes don't excite me.

T   F   2. I feel I can trust my friends.

T   F   3. Small imperfections in a person are rarely enough to change my love into hatred.

T   F   4. There have been times when I have hated one or both of my parents for the affection they have expressed for me.

T   F   5. Words of affection almost always make people uncomfortable.

T   F   6. I don't mind too much the faults of people I admire.

T   F   7. Love and hate tend to go together.

T   F   8. Honest people will tell you that they often feel chronic resentment toward the people they love.

T   F   9. Everything I enjoy has its painful side.

T   F   10. Love never seems to last very long.

T   F   11. My strongest feelings of pleasure usually seem to be mixed with pain.

T   F   12. Whenever I get what I want, I usually don't want it at all any more.

T   F   13. I have always experienced dissatisfaction with feelings of love.

T   F   14. I worry the most when things are going the best.

T   F   15. I often get very angry with people just because I love them so much.

T   F   16. I start distrusting people if I have to depend on them too much.

T   F   17. I can think of someone right now whom I thought I liked a day or two ago, but now strongly dislike.

T   F   18. The people around me seem to be very changeable.

T   F   19. It is hard to imagine two people loving one another for many years.

T   F   20. The closer I get to people, the more I am annoyed by their faults.

T   F   21. I find that the surest way to start resenting someone is to just start liking him or her too much.

T   F   22. Often I feel as if I hate even my favorite activities.

T   F   23. I usually know when I can trust someone.

T   F   24. Everyone has a lot of hidden resentment toward his or her loved ones.

T   F   25. I usually know exactly how I feel about people I have grown close to.

T   F   26. I have noticed that feelings of tenderness often turn into feelings of anger.

T   F   27. I always seem to be the most unsure of myself at the same time that I am most confident of myself.

T   F   28. My interest in personally enjoyed hobbies and pastimes has remained relatively stable.

T   F   29. I can usually depend on those with whom I am close.

T   F   30. My experiences with love have always been muddled with great frustration.

T   F   31. I usually find that feelings of hate will interfere when I have grown to love someone.

T   F   32. A sense of shame has often interfered with my accepting words of praise from others.

T   F   33. I rarely feel rejected by those who depend on me.

T   F   34. I am wary of love becuse it is such a short-lived emotion.

T   F   35. I usually experience doubt when I have accomplished something that I have worked on for a long time.

T   F   36. I rarely doubt the appropriateness of praise that I have received from others in the past.

T   F   37. I often feel as though I cannot trust people whom I have grown to depend on.

T   F   38. I usually experience some grief over my own feelings of pleasure.

T   F   39. It is rare for me to love a person one minute and hate him or her the next minute.

T   F   40. I doubt if I can ever be sure exactly what my true interests are.

T   F   41. I can't remember ever feeling love and hate for the same person at the same time.

T   F   42. Love is always painful for me.

T   F   43. Close relationships never seem to last long.

T   F   44. I never had much trouble telling whether my parents loved me or hated me.

T   F   45. Most people disappoint their friends.

Internal Versus External Control of Weight Scale (IECW)

Chapter Link

This scale is to be used in conjunction with the Body Image chapter of *Helping the Struggling Adolescent*.

Rapid Assessment Description

This scale is designed to measure the degree to which a person considers the achievement of controlling one's weight as contingent or noncontingent on one's behavior.

Scoring Procedure

Items are arranged in a forced-choice format: One alternative reflects an internal orientation; the other, an external orientation. External choices (the first alternative in items 1, 3, and 5 and the second alternative in items 2 and 4) are scored 1. Total scores are the sum of the internal alternatives selected by the respondent. Scores range from 0 to 5.

Permission

Copyright © 1977 by the American Psychological Association. Reprinted by permission.

Available from the American Psychological Association, 1200 17th Street, N.W., Washington, DC 20036.

IECW

Each item consists of two statements. Choose the statement with which you agree most.

___ 1. a. Overweight problems are mainly a result of hereditary or physiological factors.
   b. Overweight problems are mainly a result of lack of self-control.

___ 2. a. Overweight people will lose weight only when they can generate enough internal motivation.
   b. Overweight people need some tangible external motivation in order to reduce.

___ 3. a. Diet pills can be a valuable aid in weight reduction.
   b. A person who loses weight with diet pills will gain the weight back eventually.

___ 4. a. In overweight people, hunger is caused by the expectation of being hungry.
   b. In overweight people, hunger is caused by stomach contractions and low blood sugar levels.

___ 5. a. Overweight problems can be traced to early childhood and are very resistant to change.
   b. Overweight problems can be traced to poor eating habits which are relatively simple to change.

Inventory of Religious Belief (IRB)

Chapter Link

This scale is to be used in conjunction with the Spiritual Doubt chapter of *Helping the Struggling Adolescent.*

Rapid Assessment Description

This scale is designed to differentiate between those who believe and those who reject Christian dogma.

Scoring Procedure

Eight of the statements (2, 3, 6, 7, 9, 11, 12, 15) are positively scored; seven (1, 4, 5, 8, 10, 13, 14) are reverse-scored (a high score for disagreement rather than agreement). The total score is obtained by summing the items. There is a possible range of 15 (strongest nonbeliefs) to 75 (strongest beliefs).

Permission

From *Measures in Social Psychologic Attitudes.* Copyright © 1991, Academic Press. Reprinted with permission.

Available from John P. Robinson and Phillip R. Shaver, Survey Research Center, Institute for Social Research, The University of Michigan, Ann Arbor, MI 48106.

IRB

This is a study of religious belief. Indicate on the line at the left the answer that applies best to each of the numbered statements.

5 = Strongly agree
4 = Agree
3 = Not sure
2 = Disagree
1 = Strongly disagree

Remember to read each statement carefully, and mark only one answer for each item. People differ widely in beliefs; please indicate your own in the manner described.

_____ 1. It makes no difference whether one is a Christian or not as long as one has good will for others.

_____ 2. I believe that the Bible is the inspired Word of God.

_____ 3. God created people separate and distinct from animals.

_____ 4. The idea of God is unnecessary in our enlightened age.

_____ 5. There is no life after death.

_____ 6. I believe Jesus was born of a virgin.

_____ 7. God exists as Father, Son, and Holy Spirit.

_____ 8. The Bible is full of errors, misconceptions, and contradictions.

_____ 9. The gospel of Christ is the only way for humankind to be saved.

_____10. I think there have been many people in history just as great as Jesus.

_____11. I believe there is a heaven and a hell.

_____12. Eternal life is a gift of God given only to those who believe in Jesus Christ as Savior and Lord.

_____13. I think a person can be happy and enjoy life without believing in God.

_____14. In many ways the Bible has held back and retarded human progress.

_____15. I believe in the personal, visible return of Christ to earth.

Michigan Alcoholism Screening Test (MAST)

Chapter Link

This scale is to be used in conjunction with the Drugs and Alcohol chapter of *Helping the Struggling Adolescent.*

Rapid Assessment Description

This scale is designed to detect alcoholism.

Scoring Procedure

Each item on the MAST is assigned a weight of 0 to 5, with 5 considered diagnostic of alcoholism. Weights for the items are listed in the column to the left of the numbered questions. Negative responses to items 1, 4, 6, and 8 are considered alcoholic responses; positive responses to other items are considered alcoholic responses. An overall score of 3 points or less is considered to indicate nonalcoholism, 4 points is suggestive of alcoholism, and 5 points or more indicates alcoholism.

Permission

From the *American Journal of Psychiatry* 127:89–94. Copyright © 1971, the American Psychiatric Association. Reprinted by permission.

Available from the American Psychiatric Association, 1400 K Street, N.W., Washington, DC 20005.

MAST

Please circle either yes or no for each item as it applies to you.

Yes No (2) 1. Do you feel you are a normal drinker?

Yes No (2) 2. Have you ever awakened the morning after some drinking the night before and found that you could not remember a part of the evening before?

Yes No (1) 3. Does your wife (or do your parents) ever worry or complain about your drinking?

Yes No (2) 4. Can you stop drinking without a struggle after one or two drinks?

Yes No (1) 5. Do you ever feel bad about your drinking?

Yes No (2) 6. Do friends or relatives think you are a normal drinker?

Yes No (0) 7. Do you ever try to limit your drinking to certain times of the day or to a certain place?

Yes No (2) 8. Are you always able to stop drinking when you want to?

Yes No (5) 9. Have you ever attended a meeting of Alcoholics Anonymous (AA)?

Yes No (1) 10. Have you gotten into fights when drinking?

Yes No (2) 11. Has drinking ever created problems with you and your wife?

Yes No (2) 12. Has your wife (or other family member) ever gone to anyone for help about your drinking?

Yes No (2) 13. Have you ever lost friends or girlfriends/boyfriends because of drinking?

Yes No (2) 14. Have you ever gotten into trouble at work because of drinking?

Yes No (2) 15. Have you ever lost a job because of drinking?

Yes No (2) 16. Have you ever neglected your obligations, your family, or your work for two or more days in a row because you were drinking?

Yes No (1) 17. Do you ever drink before noon?

Yes No (2) 18. Have you ever been told you have liver trouble?

Yes No (5) 19. Have you ever had delirium tremens (DTs), had severe shaking, heard voices, or seen things that weren't there after heavy drinking?

Yes No (5) 20. Have you ever gone to anyone for help about your drinking?

Yes No (5) 21. Have you ever been in a hospital because of drinking?

Yes   No   (2)   22. Have you ever been a patient in a psychiatric hospital or on a psychiatric ward of a general hospital where drinking was part of the problem?

Yes   No   (2)   23. Have you ever been seen at a psychiatric or mental health clinic, or gone to a doctor, social worker, or clergyman for help with an emotional problem in which drinking had played a part?

Yes   No   (2)   24. Have you ever been arrested, even for a few hours, because of drunk behavior?

Yes   No   (2)   25. Have you ever been arrested for drunk driving after drinking?

Mobility Inventory for Agoraphobia (MIA)

Chapter Link

This inventory is to be used in conjunction with the Phobia chapter of *Helping the Struggling Adolescent*.

Rapid Assessment Description

This instrument is designed to measure agoraphobic avoidance behavior. The MIA provides clinically useful information both in total score form and in interpretation of scores on individual items.

Scoring Procedure

Each item on the MIA is scored on a basis of 1 to 5, and each item can be interpreted independently.

Permission

Reprinted with permission from *Behavioral Research and Therapy* 23:35–44, D. L. Chambless, G. C. Caputo, S. E. Jasin, E. J. Gracely, and C. Williams, "The Mobility Inventory for Agoraphobia," copyright © 1985, Pergamon Press, Inc.

Available from Andrew Adler, Journals Permissions, 395 Saw Mill River Road, Elmsford, NY 10523.

MIA

Please indicate the degree to which you avoid the following places or situations because of discomfort or anxiety. Do this by using the following scale.

1 = Never avoid
2 = Rarely avoid
3 = Avoid about half the time
4 = Avoid most of the time
5 = Always avoid

_____ 1. Theaters
_____ 2. Supermarkets
_____ 3. Classrooms
_____ 4. Department stores
_____ 5. Restaurants
_____ 6. Museums
_____ 7. Elevators
_____ 8. Auditoriums or stadiums
_____ 9. Parking garages
_____10. High places
_____11. Enclosed places (e.g., tunnels)
_____12. Open spaces (e.g., fields)

Riding in—
_____13. Buses
_____14. Trains
_____15. Subways
_____16. Airplanes
_____17. Boats

Driving or riding in car—
_____18. At any time
_____19. On expressways

Situations:
_____20. Standing in lines
_____21. Crossing bridges
_____22. Parties or social gatherings
_____23. Walking on the street
_____24. Being far away from home

Novaco Anger Scale (NAS)

Chapter Link

This scale is to be used in conjunction with the Anger, Forgiveness, and Siblings chapters of *Helping the Struggling Adolescent*.

Rapid Assessment Description

This scale is designed to measure the intensity of a person's anger.

Scoring Procedure

Add the scores for the 25 items. Scores range from 0 to 100, with a higher score indicating a more intense struggle with the emotion of anger. Scores can be interpreted according to the following scale:

0–45   The amount of anger this person generally experiences is remarkably low. Only a few percent of the population will score this low on the test.

46–55   These people are substantially more peaceful than the average person.

56–75   These people respond to life's annoyances with an average amount of anger.

76–85   These people frequently react in an angry way to life's many annoyances. They are substantially more irritable than the average person.

86–100   These people are true anger champions and as such are plagued by frequent, intense, and furious reactions that do not quickly disappear. They probably harbor negative feelings long after the incident has passed. They may have the reputation of being a firecracker or a hothead, among others.

Permission

Reprinted with permission from Dr. Raymond W. Novaco.

Available from Raymond W. Novaco, Program in Social Ecology, University of California–Irvine, Irvine, CA 92717.

NAS

Read the following list of twenty-five potentially upsetting situations. In the space provided, estimate the degree to which each incident would ordinarily anger or provoke you. Use this rating scale:

> 0 = You would feel very little or no annoyance.
> 1 = You would feel a little irritated.
> 2 = You would feel moderately upset.
> 3 = You would feel quite angry.
> 4 = You would feel very angry.

Mark your answer before each question, as in this example:

__2__   I feel that people would not like me if they really knew me well.

The person who answered this question estimated his reaction as a 2 because he would feel moderately irritated, but this would quickly pass as soon as the moment was gone. As you describe how you would ordinarily react to each of the following provocations, make your best general estimate even though many potentially important details are omitted (such as what kind of day you were having, who was involved in the situation, etc.).

_____ 1. You unpack an appliance you have just bought, plug it in, and discover that it doesn't work.

_____ 2. You are overcharged by a repairman who has you over a barrel.

_____ 3. You are singled out for correction while the actions of others go unnoticed.

_____ 4. You get stuck in your family's car in the mud or snow.

_____ 5. You are talking to someone, and he or she doesn't answer you.

_____ 6. Someone pretends to be something he or she is not.

_____ 7. While you are struggling to carry four cups of Coke to your table in the cafeteria, someone bumps into you, spilling the Coke.

_____ 8. You have hung up your clothes, but someone knocks them to the floor and fails to pick them up.

_____ 9. You are hounded by a salesperson from the moment you walk into a store.

_____ 10. You have made arrangements to go somewhere with a person who backs out at the last minute and leaves you hanging.

_____ 11. You are joked with or teased.

_____ 12. You are in your car, and it is stalled at a traffic light, and the driver behind you keeps blowing his horn.

_____ 13. You are learning to drive and accidentally make the wrong kind of turn in a parking lot. As you get out of your car, someone yells at you, "Where did you learn to drive?"

_____ 14. Someone makes a mistake and blames it on you.

_____ 15. You are trying to concentrate, but a person near you is tapping his or her foot.

_____ 16. You lend someone an important book or tool, and he or she fails to return it.

_____ 17. You have had a busy day, and your mom or dad starts to complain about how you forgot to do something you agreed to do.

_____ 18. You are trying to discuss something important with a friend who isn't giving you a chance to express your feelings.

_____ 19. You are in a discussion with someone who persists in arguing about a topic he or she knows very little about.

_____ 20. Someone sticks his or her nose into an argument between you and someone else.

_____ 21. You need to get somewhere quickly, but the car in front of you is going 25 mph in a 40 mph zone, and you or the driver of your car is unable to pass.

_____ 22. You step on a gob of chewing gum.

_____ 23. You are mocked by a small group of people as you pass them.

_____ 24. In a hurry to get somewhere, you tear a good pair of slacks on a sharp object.

_____ 25. You use your last dime to make a phone call, but you are disconnected before you finish dialing, and the dime is lost.

Obsessive–Compulsive Scale (OCS)

Chapter Link

This scale is to be used in conjunction with the Obsessions and Compulsions chapter of *Helping the Struggling Adolescent*.

Rapid Assessment Description

This scale is designed to measure the respondent's general tendency toward obsessive thoughts and compulsive behaviors.

Scoring Procedure

Items 1, 2, 4, 6, 7, 8, 16, 17, 18, and 21 are assigned 1 point if answered *True*. Items 5, 9, 10, 11, 12, 13, 14, 19, 20, and 22 are assigned 1 point if answered *False*. Scores range from 0 to 20, with higher scores indicating more compulsivity. Items 3 and 15 are validity checks, and if they are answered incorrectly, the OCS scores should not be considered valid.

Permission

Reprinted with permission from Gerald D. Gibb.

Available from LCDR Gerald D. Gibb, MSC, USNR, Chief of Naval Personnel, Pers 312-D, Washington, DC 20370.

OCS

Please indicate whether each statement below is true or false for you by circling the T or the F to the left of the question.

T F   1. I feel compelled to do things I don't want to do.

T F   2. I usually check things that I know I have already done.

T F   3. I can walk 30 miles in an hour.

T F   4. I often do things I don't want to do because I cannot resist doing them.

T F   5. I seldom keep a daily routine.

T F   6. I feel compelled always to complete what I am doing.

T F   7. I often feel the need to double-check what I do.

T F   8. I'd rather do things the same way all the time.

T F   9. I seldom have recurring thoughts.

T F   10. I seldom am compelled to do something I don't want to do.

T F   11. I don't feel uncomfortable and uneasy when I don't do things my usual way.

T F   12. If I don't feel like doing something, it won't bother me not to do it.

T F   13. I usually never feel the need to be organized.

T F   14. I am uneasy about keeping a rigid time schedule.

T F   15. My birthday comes once a year.

T F   16. I am often compelled to do some things I do not want to do.

T F   17. I like to keep a rigid daily routine.

T F   18. I believe there is a place for everything and everything in its place.

T F   19. I seldom check things I know I have already done.

T F   20. I am not obsessed with details.

T F   21. I often have recurring thoughts.

T F   22. I like to do things differently each time.

Reasons for Living Inventory (RLI)

Chapter Link

This inventory is to be used in conjunction with the Suicide chapter of *Helping the Struggling Adolescent*.

Rapid Assessment Description

This measure assesses a range of beliefs that differentiate suicidal from nonsuicidal persons.

Scoring Procedure

The RLI is scored by summing each item score and dividing by 20. Higher scores indicate more reasons for living and a lower risk of attempting suicide. The average score for nonsuicidal individuals is 4.25.

Permission

Reprinted with permission from the *Journal of Consulting and Clinical Psychology* 51, M. M. Linehan, J. L. Goldstein, S. L. Neilsen, and J. A. Chiles, "Reasons for Staying Alive When You Are Thinking of Killing Yourself: The Reason for Living Inventory," copyright © 1983.

Available from Dr. Marsha M. Linehan, Department of Psychology NI-25, University of Washington, Seattle, WA 98195.

RLI

Many people have thought of suicide at least once. Others have never considered it. Whether you have considered it or not, we are interested in the reasons you would have for not committing suicide if the thought were to occur to you or if someone were to suggest it to you.

Below are reasons people sometimes give for not committing suicide. We would like to know how important each of these possible reasons would be to you at this time in your life as a reason not to kill yourself. Please rate these in the space at the left on each question.

In each space put a number to indicate the importance to you of each reason for not killing yourself.

1 = Not at all important
2 = Quite unimportant
3 = Somewhat unimportant
4 = Somewhat important
5 = Quite important
6 = Extremely important

_____ 1. I have a responsibility and commitment to my family.

_____ 2. I believe I can learn to adjust or cope with my problems.

_____ 3. I believe I have control over my life and destiny.

_____ 4. I have a desire to live.

_____ 5. I believe only God has the right to end a life.

_____ 6. I am afraid of death.

_____ 7. My family might believe I did not love them.

_____ 8. I do not believe that things get hopeless enough that I would rather be dead.

_____ 9. My family depends upon me and needs me.

_____10. I am afraid of the actual "act" of killing myself (the pain, blood, violence).

_____11. I have future plans I am looking forward to carrying out.

_____12. Life is all we have and is better than nothing.

_____13. No matter how bad I feel, I know that it will not last.

_____14. I am afraid of the unknown.

_____15. I want to experience all that life has to offer.

_____16. I am afraid that my method of killing myself would fail.

____17. I am afraid of going to hell.

____18. I would not want my family to feel guilty afterwards.

____19. I am concerned what others would think of me.

____20. My religious beliefs forbid it.

Restraint Scale (RS)

Chapter Link

This scale is to be used in conjunction with the Eating Disorders chapter of *Helping the Struggling Adolescent*.

Rapid Assessment Description

This scale is designed to measure one aspect of dieting behavior, the ability to restrain from eating in order to maintain a particular weight. The scale ranges from the extreme of someone who has never given a moment's thought about dieting to someone who is overly concerned with dieting. The instrument may be useful with both obese clients attempting to reduce weight and with anorexic and bulimic clients.

Scoring Procedure

The RS score is the sum of all ten items. For items 1–4 and 10, the alternatives are scored as follows: $a = 0, b = 1, c = 2, d = 3, e = 4$. Items 5 – 9 are scored as follows: $a = 0, b = 1, c = 2, d = 3$. Scores range from 0 to 35, with higher scores indicating more concern over dieting.

Permission

Reprinted with permission from C. Peter Herman.

Available from Dr. C. Peter Herman, Department of Psychology, University of Toronto, Toronto, Ontario, M5S 1A1, Canada.

RS

Please answer the following items using the alternatives provided.

___ 1. How often are you dieting?
   a. Never   b. Rarely   c. Sometimes   d. Often   e. Always

___ 2. What is the maximum amount of weight (in pounds) that you have ever lost in one month?
   a. 0−4   b. 5−9   c. 10−14   d. 15−19   e. 20+

___ 3. What is your maximum weight gain within a week?
   a. 0−1   b. 1.1−2   c. 2.1−3   d. 3.1−5   e. 5.1+

___ 4. In a typical week, how much does your weight fluctuate?
   a. 0−1   b. 1.1−2   c. 2.1−3   d. 3.1−5   e. 5.1+

___ 5. Would a weight fluctuation of five pounds affect the way you live your life?
   a. Not at all   b. Slightly   c. Moderately   d. Very much

___ 6. Do you eat sensibly in front of others and splurge alone?
   a. Never   b. Rarely   c. Often   d. Always

___ 7. Do you give too much time and thought to food?
   a. Never   b. Rarely   c. Often   d. Always

___ 8. Do you have feelings of guilt after overeating?
   a. Never   b. Rarely   c. Often   d. Always

___ 9. How conscious are you of what you are eating?
   a. Not at all   b. Slightly   c. Moderately   d. Extremely

___10. How many pounds over your desired weight were you at your maximum weight?
   a. 0−1   b. 2−5   c. 6−10   d. 11−20   e. 21+

Revised UCLA Loneliness Scale (RULS)

Chapter Link

This scale is to be used in conjunction with the Loneliness chapter of *Helping the Struggling Adolescent*.

Rapid Assessment Description

This scale is designed to measure loneliness in a variety of populations. The scale identifies loneliness as a problem in and of itself or as related to other problems.

Scoring Procedure

After reverse-scoring items 1, 4, 5, 6, 9, 10, 15, 16, 19, 20, and 21, sum the scores on all twenty items to produce a possible range of scores from 20 to 80, with higher scores indicating greater loneliness.

Permission

Reprinted with permission, *Journal of Personality and Social Psychology* 39, D. Russell, L. A. Peplau, and C. E. Cutrona, "The Revised UCLA Loneliness Scale: Concurrent and Discriminant Validity Evidence," copyright © 1980.

Available from Professor Letitia A. Paplau, Department of Psychology, University of California at Los Angeles (UCLA), Los Angeles, CA 90024.

RULS

Indicate how often you have felt the way described in each statement, using the following scale:

4 = "I have felt this way often."
3 = "I have felt this way sometimes."
2 = "I have felt this way rarely."
1 = "I have never felt this way."

___ 1. I feel in tune with the people around me.

___ 2. I lack companionship.

___ 3. There is no one I can turn to.

___ 4. I do not feel alone.

___ 5. I feel part of a group of friends.

___ 6. I have a lot in common with the people around me.

___ 7. I am no longer close to anyone.

___ 8. My interests and ideas are not shared by those around me.

___ 9. I am an outgoing person.

___10. There are people I feel close to.

___11. I feel left out.

___12. My social relationships are superficial.

___13. No one really knows me well.

___14. I feel isolated from others.

___15. I can find companionship when I want it.

___16. There are people who really understand me.

___17. I am unhappy being so withdrawn.

___18. People are around me but not with me.

___19. There are people I can talk to.

___20. There are people I can turn to.

Self-Efficacy Scale (SES)

Chapter Link

This scale is to be used in conjunction with the Inferiority chapter of *Helping the Struggling Adolescent*.

Rapid Assessment Description

This scale is designed to measure general expectations of self-efficacy that are not tied to specific situations or behavior. The scale assumes that personal expectations of mastery are a major determinant of behavioral change. This scale may be useful in tailoring the course of counseling to the young person's needs, and it can also be used as an index of progress, since expectations of self-efficacy should change during the course of counseling.

Scoring Procedure

Seven items (1, 5, 9, 13, 17, 21, 25) are filler items and are not scored. After items presented in a negative fashion (3, 6, 7, 8, 11, 14, 18, 20, 22, 24, 26, 29, 30) are reverse-scored, the scores for all items are summed. Before reverse-scoring, the answers are keyed as follows: $A = 1, B = 2, C = 3, D = 4, E = 5$. The higher the score, the higher the self-efficacy expectations.

Permission

Reproduced with permission of authors and publishers from M. Sherer, J. E. Maddux, B. Mercandante, S. Prentice-Dunn, B. Jacobs, and R. W. Rogers, "The Self-Efficacy Scale: Construction and Validation," *Psychological Reports*, 1982, 51:663–71, and *Psychological Reports*, 1982.

Available from Dr. Mark Sherer, 1874 Pleasant Avenue, Mobile, AL 36617.

SES

This questionnaire is a series of statements about your personal attitudes and traits. Each statement represents a commonly held belief. Read each statement and decide to what extent it describes you. There are no right or wrong answers. You will probably agree with some of the statements and disagree with others. Please indicate your personal feelings about each statement below by marking the letter that best describes your attitude or feeling. Please be very truthful and describe yourself as you really are, not as you would like to be.

> A = Disagree strongly
> B = Disagree moderately
> C = Neither agree nor disagree
> D = Agree moderately
> E = Agree strongly

____ 1. I like to grow house plants.

____ 2. When I make plans, I am certain I can make them work.

____ 3. One of my problems is that I cannot get down to work when I should.

____ 4. If I can't do a job the first time, I keep trying until I can.

____ 5. Heredity plays the major role in determining one's personality.

____ 6. It is difficult for me to make new friends.

____ 7. When I set important goals for myself, I rarely achieve them.

____ 8. I give up on things before completing them.

____ 9. I like to cook.

____10. If I see someone I would like to meet, I go to that person instead of waiting for him or her to come to me.

____11. I avoid facing difficulties.

____12. If something looks too complicated, I will not even bother to try it.

____13. There is some good in everybody.

____14. If I meet someone interesting who is very hard to make friends with, I'll soon stop trying to make friends with that person.

____15. When I have something unpleasant to do, I stick to it until I finish it.

____16. When I decide to do something, I go right to work on it.

____17. I like science.

____18. When trying to learn something new, I soon give up if I am not initially successful.

____19. When I'm trying to become friends with someone who seems uninterested at first, I don't give up very easily.

____20. When unexpected problems occur, I don't handle them well.

____21. If I were an artist, I would like to draw children.

_____22. I avoid trying to learn new things when they look too difficult for me.

_____23. Failure just makes me try harder.

_____24. I do not handle myself well in social gatherings.

_____25. I very much like to ride horses.

_____26. I feel insecure about my ability to do things.

_____27. I am a self-reliant person.

_____28. I have acquired my friends through my personal abilities at making friends.

_____29. I give up easily.

_____30. I do not seem capable of dealing with most problems that come up in my life.

Self-Rating Anxiety Scale (SAS)

Chapter Link

This scale is to be used in conjunction with the Anxiety chapter of *Helping the Struggling Adolescent.*

Rapid Assessment Description

This scale is designed to evaluate the level of anxiety based on the most commonly found characteristics of an anxiety disorder. Five items focus on affective symptoms and fifteen items focus on somatic symptoms.

Scoring Procedure

The SAS is scored by summing the values on each item to produce a raw score ranging from 20 to 80. An SAS index is derived by dividing the raw score by 80, producing an index that ranges from .25 to 1.00. Higher scores indicate more anxiety.

Permission

Reprinted with permission from *Psychosomatics* 12:371–79, W. K. Zung, "A Rating Instrument for Anxiety Disorders," copyright © 1971 by Psykey, Inc.

Available from Psykey, Inc., Permissions Office, 7750 Daggett Street, San Diego, CA 92111.

SAS

Below are twenty statements. Please rate each using the following scale:

1 = Some or a little of the time
2 = Some of the time
3 = Good part of the time
4 = Most or all of the time

Please record your rating in the space to the left of each item.

_____ 1. I feel more nervous and anxious than usual.

_____ 2. I feel afraid for no reason at all.

_____ 3. I get upset easily or feel panicky.

_____ 4. I feel as if I'm falling apart and going to pieces.

_____ 5. I feel that everything is all right amd nothing bad will happen.

_____ 6. My arms and legs shake and tremble.

_____ 7. I am bothered by headaches and neck and back pains.

_____ 8. I feel weak and get tired easily.

_____ 9. I feel calm and can sit still easily.

_____10. I can feel my heart beating fast.

_____11. I am bothered by dizzy spells.

_____12. I have fainting spells or feel like it.

_____13. I can breathe in and out easily.

_____14. I get a feeling of numbness and tingling in my fingers, toes.

_____15. I am bothered by stomach aches or indigestion.

_____16. I have to empty my bladder often.

_____17. My hands are usually dry and warm.

_____18. My face gets hot and blushes.

_____19. I fall asleep easily and get a good night's rest.

_____20. I have nightmares.

Self-Rating Depression Scale (SDS)

Chapter Link

This scale is to be used in conjunction with the Depression and Suicide chapters of *Helping the Struggling Adolescent*.

Rapid Assessment Description

This scale is designed to assess depression as a disorder and quantify the symptoms of depression.

Scoring Procedure

The SDS is scored by summing the values on each item to produce a raw score ranging from 20 to 80. An SDS index is derived by dividing the raw score by 80 to produce an index that ranges from .25 to 1.00 (higher scores equaling higher depression).

Permission

Reprinted with permission from *Archives of General Psychiatry* 12:63–70, W. K. Zung, "A Self-Rating Depression Scale," copyright © 1965, American Medical Association.

Available from Psykey, Inc., 7750 Daggett Street, San Diego, CA 92111.

SDS

Below are twenty statements. Please rate each using the following scale:

    1 = Some or a little of the time
    2 = Some of the time
    3 = Good part of the time
    4 = Most or all of the time

Please record your rating in the space to the left of each item.

_____ 1. I feel downhearted, blue, and sad.

_____ 2. Mornings are when I feel best.

_____ 3. I have crying spells or feel like it.

_____ 4. I have trouble sleeping through the night.

_____ 5. I eat as much as I used to.

_____ 6. I enjoy looking at, talking to, and being with attractive women/men.

_____ 7. I notice that I am losing weight.

_____ 8. I have trouble with constipation.

_____ 9. My heart beats faster than usual.

_____10. I get tired for no reason.

_____11. My mind is as clear as it used to be.

_____12. I find it easy to do the things I used to.

_____13. I am restless and I can't keep still.

_____14. I feel hopeful about the future.

_____15. I am more irritable than usual.

_____16. I find it easy to make decisions.

_____17. I feel that I am useful and needed.

_____18. My life is pretty full.

_____19. I feel that others would be better off if I were dead.

_____20. I still enjoy the things I used to.

Skills for Classroom Success Checklist (SCSC)

Chapter Link

This checklist is to be used in conjunction with the School Work chapter of *Helping the Struggling Adolescent*.

Rapid Assessment Description

This checklist is designed to show how well a person performs in areas that are necessary to classroom success.

Scoring Procedure

There are no scores or answers for this checklist; it simply shows what areas of classroom skills need improvement.

Permission

The SCSC is available from Research Press, 2612 North Mattis Avenue, Champaign, IL 61821. Copyright © 1990 by Rosemarie S. Morganett. Reprinted by permission.

SCSC

Instructions: Below are several skills that are important for doing well in class. Read each item, then circle the number of the response that is most like you at this time.
Scale:

1 = I do very well
2 = I do well
3 = I do OK
4 = I need to improve some
5 = I need to improve a lot

1. I go to every class and get there on time.	1	2	3	4	5
2. I take a notebook to every class.	1	2	3	4	5
3. I listen and concentrate in class.	1	2	3	4	5
4. I ask questions when I need information.	1	2	3	4	5
5. I take good notes in class.	1	2	3	4	5
6. I listen for possible test questions.	1	2	3	4	5
7. I participate actively in class.	1	2	3	4	5
8. I understand what it will take to complete homework assignments.	1	2	3	4	5
9. I have a "study buddy" in each class.	1	2	3	4	5
10. I practice good stress management before and after class.	1	2	3	4	5

Skills for Study Success Checklist (SSSC)

Chapter Link

This checklist is to be used in conjunction with the School Work chapter of *Helping the Struggling Adolescent.*

Rapid Assessment Description

This checklist is designed to help the respondent see what areas need improvement in order to have effective and successful study practices.

Scoring Procedure

This checklist is not tabulated or scored. It can be used to help the young person identify areas that need improvement for study success.

Permission

The SSSC is available from Research Press, 2612 North Mattis Avenue, Champaign, IL 61821. Copyright © 1990 by Rosemarie S. Morganett. Reprinted by permission.

SSSC

Instructions: Below are several skills that have to do with studying. Read each item, then circle the number of the response that is most like you at this time.

Scale:

1 = I do very well
2 = I do well
3 = I do OK
4 = I need to improve some
5 = I need to improve a lot

1. I am aware of my own learning style.	1	2	3	4	5
2. I set goals for my study time.	1	2	3	4	5
3. I take good notes during class.	1	2	3	4	5
4. I carefully reread my class notes.	1	2	3	4	5
5. I have effective reading skills.	1	2	3	4	5
6. I know how to study a chapter effectively.	1	2	3	4	5
7. I study regularly.	1	2	3	4	5
8. I use my study time at school effectively.	1	2	3	4	5
9. I spend enough time studying.	1	2	3	4	5
10. I plan a reward for myself after studying.	1	2	3	4	5

Stanford Shyness Survey (SSS)

Chapter Link

This survey is to be used in conjunction with the Shyness chapter of *Helping the Struggling Adolescent*.

Rapid Assessment Description

This measure is designed to assess a person's proneness to shyness.

Scoring Procedure

This assessment tool is used to provide a baseline against which to evaluate later changes in shyness that result from implementing the techniques described in the Shyness chapter in *Helping the Struggling Adolescent*. It is best used by administering early in treatment, a month later, six months later, and a year from beginning counseling.

Permission

Copyright © by Dr. Philip Zimbardo of Stanford University. Reprinted by permission.

Available from Philip G. Zimbardo, Ph.D., Department of Psychology, Stanford University, Stanford, CA 94305.

SSS

For each question, circle the letter preceding the response that best fits you at this time.

1. Do you consider yourself a shy person?
   a. Yes
   b. No

2. If yes, have you always been shy (were shy previously and still are)?
   a. Yes
   b. No

3. If no to question 1, was there *ever* a prior time in your life when you were shy?
   a. Yes
   b. No

If no, then you are finished with this survey. Thanks. If yes to any of the above, please continue.

4. *How shy* are you when you feel shy?
   a. Extremely shy
   b. Very shy
   c. Quite shy
   d. Moderately shy
   e. Somewhat shy
   f. Only slightly shy

5. How *often* do you experience (have you experienced) these feelings of shyness?
   a. Every day
   b. Almost every day
   c. Often; nearly every other day
   d. One or two times a week
   e. Occasionally; less than once a week
   f. Rarely; once a month or less

6. Compared with your peers (people of similar age, sex, and background), how shy are you?
   a. Much more shy
   b. More shy
   c. About as shy
   d. Less shy
   e. Much less shy

7. How *desirable* is it for you to be shy?
   a. Very undesirable
   b. Undesirable
   c. Neither
   d. Desirable
   e. Very desirable

8. Is (or was) your shyness ever a personal *problem* for you?
   a. Yes, often
   b. Yes, sometimes

    c. Yes, occasionally
    d. Rarely
    e. Never

9. When you are feeling shy, can you *conceal* it and have others believe you are not feeling shy?
    a. Yes, always
    b. Sometimes I can, sometimes not
    c. No, I usually cannot hide it

10. Do you consider yourself more of an *introvert* or an *extrovert*?
    a. Strongly introverted
    b. Moderately introverted
    c. Slightly introverted
    d. Neither
    e. Slightly extroverted
    f. Moderately extroverted
    g. Strongly extroverted

(11–19) *Which of the following do you believe may be among the causes of your shyness? Check all that are applicable to you.*

11. Concern for negative evaluation

12. Fear of being rejected

13. Lack of self-confidence

14. Lack of specific social skills (specify): _____
_____

15. Fear of being intimate with others

16. Preference for being alone

17. Value placed on nonsocial interests, hobbies, etc.

18. Personal inadequacy, handicap (specify): _____
_____

19. Others (specify): _____
_____

(20–27) *Perceptions of your shyness: Do the following people consider you to be shy? How shy do you think they judge you to be? Answer using this scale:*

        1 = Extremely shy
        2 = Very shy
        3 = Quite shy
        4 = Moderately shy
        5 = Somewhat shy
        6 = Only slightly shy
        7 = Not shy
        8 = Don't know
        9 = Not applicable

____20. Your mother

_____21. Your father

_____22. Your siblings (brothers and/or sisters)

_____23. Close friends

_____24. Your steady boyfriend/girlfriend/spouse

_____25. Your high-school classmates

_____26. Your current roommate

_____27. Teachers or employers, fellow workers who know you well

28. In deciding whether or not to call yourself a "shy person," was your decision based on the fact that
    a. You are (were) shy all the time in all situations
    b. You are (were) shy at least 50 percent of the time, in more situations than not
    c. You are (were) shy only occasionally, but those occasions are (were) of enough importance to justify calling yourself a shy person

29. Have people ever misinterpreted your shyness as a different trait, e.g., "indifference," "aloofness," "poise"?
    a. Yes (specify): _____

    _____
    b. No

30. Do you ever feel shy when you are *alone?*
    a. Yes
    b. No

31. Do you ever feel *embarrassed* when you are alone?
    a. Yes
    b. No

32. If yes, please describe when, how, or why: _____

    _____

    _____

(33–36) *What makes you shy?*

33. If you now experience, or have ever experienced, feelings of shyness, please indicate which of the following situations, activities, and types of people make you feel shy. (Place a check mark next to *all* the appropriate choices.)

Situations and activities that make me feel shy:
- ☐ Social situations in general
- ☐ Large groups
- ☐ Small, task-oriented groups (e.g., seminars at school, work groups on the job)
- ☐ Small, social groups (e.g., at parties, dances)
- ☐ One-to-one interactions with a person of the same sex
- ☐ One-to-one interactions with a person of the opposite sex
- ☐ Situations where I am vulnerable (e.g., when asking for help)

☐ Situations where I am of lower status than others (e.g., when speaking to superiors, authorities)

☐ Situations requiring assertiveness (e.g., when complaining about faulty service in a restaurant or the poor quality of a product)

☐ Situations where I am the focus of attention before a large group (e.g., when giving a speech)

☐ Situations where I am the focus of attention before a small group (e.g., when being introduced, when being asked directly for my opinion)

☐ Situations where I am being evaluated or compared with others (e.g., when being interviewed, when being criticized)

☐ New interpersonal situations in general

34. Now please go back and indicate next to each item you checked in no. 33 whether your shyness has been elicited in the *past month* by the situation or activity:

        0 = Not in the past month, but prior
        1 = Yes, very strongly
        2 = Yes, strongly so
        3 = Moderately so
        4 = Only mildly
        5 = Not at all

35. Types of people who make me feel shy:

☐ My parents

☐ My siblings (brothers and/or sisters)

☐ Other relatives

☐ Friends

☐ Strangers

☐ Foreigners

☐ Authorities (by virtue of their roles—police, teacher, superior at work)

☐ Authorities (by virtue of their knowledge—intellectual superiors, experts)

☐ Elderly people (much older than I)

☐ Children (much younger than I)

☐ Persons of the opposite sex, in a group

☐ Persons of the same sex, in a group

☐ A person of the opposite sex, one-to-one

☐ A person of the same sex, one-to-one

36. Now please go back and indicate next to each item you checked in no. 35 whether your shyness has been elicited in the *past month* by this person (or type of person):

        0 = Not in the past month, but prior
        1 = Yes, very strongly
        2 = Yes, strongly so
        3 = Moderately so
        4 = Only mildly

(37–40) *Shyness reactions*

37. How do you know you are shy (i.e., what *cues* do you use)?

    a. My internal feelings, thoughts, symptoms only (private)

    b. My overt behavior in a given situation only (public)

    c. A mix of internal responses and overt behavior

Physical reactions:

38. If you do experience, or have ever experienced, feelings of shyness, which of the following *physical reactions* are associated with such feelings? Put *0* next to those that are not relevant, then order the rest from *1* (most typical, usual, severe) to *2* (next most), and so on.

____ Blushing	____ Dry mouth
____ Increased pulse	____ Tremors
____ Heart pounding	____ Perspiration
____ Fatigue	____ Tingling sensations
____ Butterflies in stomach	____ Other (specify below):

Thoughts, feelings:

39. What are the specific *thoughts and sensations* associated with your shyness? Put *0* next to those that are not relevant, then order the next from *1* (most typical, usual, severe) to *2* (next most), and so on. (More than one item can be given the same rank.)

____ Positive thoughts (e.g., feeling content with myself)

____ No specific thoughts (e.g., daydreaming, thinking about nothing in particular)

____ Self-consciousness (e.g., extreme awareness of myself, of my every action)

____ Thoughts that focus on the unpleasantness of the situation (e.g., thinking that the situation is terrible, thinking that I would like to be out of the situation)

____ Thoughts that provide distractions (e.g., thinking of other things I could be doing, thinking that the experience will be over in a short while)

____ Negative thoughts about myself (e.g., feeling inadequate, insecure, inferior, stupid)

____ Thoughts about the evaluations of me that others are making (e.g., wondering what the people around me are thinking of me)

____ Thoughts about the way I am handling myself (e.g., wondering what kind of impression I am creating and how I might control it)

____ Thoughts about shyness in general (e.g., thinking about the extent of my shyness and its consequences, wishing that I were not shy)

____ Others (specify): _____

Actions:

40. If you do experience, or have ever experienced, feelings of shyness, what are the *obvious behaviors* that might indicate to others that you are feeling shy? Put *0* next to those items that are not relevant, then rank order the rest from *1* (most typical, usual, severe) to *2* (next most), and so on. (More than one item can be given the same rank.)

____ Low speaking voice   ____ Rambling, incoherent talk

____ Avoidance of other people   ____ Posture

____ Inability to make eye contact   ____ Avoidance of taking action

____ Silence (a reluctance to talk)   ____ Escape from the situation

____ Stuttering

____ Others (specify): _____

(41–42) *Shyness consequences:*

41. What are the *negative* consequences of being shy? (Check all those that apply to you.)

☐ None; no negative consequences

☐ Creates social problems; makes it difficult to meet new people, to make new friends, to enjoy potentially good experiences

☐ Has negative emotional consequences; creates feelings of loneliness, isolation, depression

☐ Prevents positive evaluations by others (e.g., my personal assets never become apparent because of my shyness)

☐ Makes it difficult to be appropriately assertive, to express opinions, to take advantage of opportunities

☐ Allows incorrect negative evaluations by others (e.g., I may unjustly be seen as unfriendly or snobbish or weak)

☐ Creates cognitive and expressive difficulties; inhibits the capacity to think clearly while with others and to communicate effectively with them

☐ Encourages excessive self-consciousness, preoccupation with myself

42. What are the *positive* consequences of being shy? (Check all those that apply to you.)

☐ None; no positive consequences

☐ Creates a modest, appealing impression; makes one appear discreet, introspective

☐ Helps avoid interpersonal conflicts

☐ Provides a convenient form of anonymity and protection

☐ Provides an opportunity to stand back, observe others, act carefully and intelligently

☐ Avoids negative evaluations by others (e.g., a shy person is not considered obnoxious, overaggressive, or pretentious)

☐ Provides a way to be selective about the people with whom one interacts

☐ Creates positive interpersonal consequences by not putting others off, intimidating them, or hurting them

43. Do you think your shyness can be overcome?
    a. Yes
    b. No
    c. Uncertain

44. Are you willing to work seriously at overcoming shyness?
    a. Yes, definitely
    b. Yes, perhaps
    c. Not sure yet
    d. No

State-Trait Anger Scale (STAS)

Chapter Link

This scale is to be used in conjunction with the Anger and Siblings chapters of *Helping the Struggling Adolescent.*

Rapid Assessment Description

This scale is designed to provide scores for two kinds of anger. State anger is specific to the moment, and trait anger pertains to how a person generally feels. A distinction between these two kinds of anger and a measure of each can be useful in working through a struggle with anger.

Scoring Procedure

The trait-anger items are rated on 4-point scales from 1 (almost never) to 4 (almost always). Scores are the sum of the item ratings. The state-anger items are rated on intensity of feelings from 1 (not at all) to 4 (very much so). Scores are the sum of the state-anger items. For both state and trait anger, scores range from 10 to 40 for the ten items.

Permission

STAS

A number of statements that people have used to describe themselves are given below. Read the statements and indicate how you generally feel by placing the appropriate number next to each item.

1 = Almost never
2 = Sometimes
3 = Often
4 = Almost always

_____ 1. I have a fiery temper.

_____ 2. I am quick tempered.

_____ 3. I am a hotheaded person.

_____ 4. I get annoyed when I am singled out for correction.

_____ 5. It makes me furious when I am criticized in front of others.

_____ 6. I get angry when I'm slowed down by others' mistakes.

_____ 7. I feel infuriated when I do a good job and get a poor evaluation.

_____ 8. I fly off the handle.

_____ 9. I feel annoyed when I am not given recognition for doing good work.

_____10. People who think they are always right irritate me.

_____11. When I get mad, I say nasty things.

_____12. I feel irritated.

_____13. I feel angry.

_____14. When I get frustrated, I feel like hitting someone.

_____15. It makes my blood boil when I am pressured.

A number of statements that people have used to describe how they feel are given below. Read the statements and indicate how you feel at the moment by placing the appropriate number next to each item.

1 = Not at all
2 = Somewhat
3 = Moderately so
4 = Very much so

_____ 1. I am mad.

_____ 2. I feel angry.

_____ 3. I am burned up.

_____ 4. I feel irritated.

_____ 5. I feel frustrated.

_____ 6. I feel aggravated.

_____ 7. I feel as if I am going to explode.

_____ 8. I feel like banging on the table.

_____ 9. I feel like yelling at somebody.
_____10. I feel like swearing.
_____11. I am furious.
_____12. I feel like hitting someone.
_____13. I feel like breaking things.
_____14. I am annoyed.
_____15. I am resentful.

Stressors Rating Scale (SRS)

Chapter Link

This scale is to be used in conjunction with the Anxiety chapter of *Helping the Struggling Adolescent*.

Rapid Assessment Description

This scale shows how much stress each of the people, places, and events listed causes the young person.

Scoring Procedure

There are no scores or answers for this checklist. It is to be used to alert the respondent to the people, situations, and places that cause stress.

Permission

The SRS is available from Research Press, 2612 North Mattis Avenue, Champaign, IL 61821. Copyright © 1990 by Rosemarie S. Morganett. Reprinted by permission.

SRS

Instructions: Circle the number that shows how much stress each of the following people, places, or events causes you. Write in the space marked Other *any stressors that aren't listed.*

Scale:

1 = No stress
2 = Slight amount of stress
3 = Moderate amount of stress
4 = A lot of stress
5 = Extremely high stress

School Stressors

1. A particular teacher   1   2   3   4   5

2. Principal   1   2   3   4   5

3. Bully   1   2   3   4   5

4. A certain subject   1   2   3   4   5

5. Feeling less smart than others   1   2   3   4   5

6. Several subjects   1   2   3   4   5

7. Worry about failing   1   2   3   4   5

8. Fear of not getting selected for a team, cheerleading, or other group   1   2   3   4   5

9. Fear of being ridiculed   1   2   3   4   5

10. Fear of not living up to parents' or teachers' expectations   1   2   3   4   5

11. Fear of not getting into a good high school or college   1   2   3   4   5

12. Fear of not knowing what to do after graduation   1   2   3   4   5

13. Other _____   1   2   3   4   5

14. Other _____   1   2   3   4   5

15. Other _____   1   2   3   4   5

Home Stressors

1. Fear of parents' divorcing   1   2   3   4   5

2. Brother's or sister's hurting me   1   2   3   4   5

3. Other family member's hurting me   1   2   3   4   5

4. Fear of parent's remarrying   1   2   3   4   5

5. Not having enough clothes or other supplies   1   2   3   4   5

6. Not getting enough attention   1   2   3   4   5

7. Having so little supervision that it is easy to get into trouble   1   2   3   4   5

8. Not getting enough affection and love   1   2   3   4   5

	1	2	3	4	5
9. Fighting between parents	1	2	3	4	5
10. Fighting with parents	1	2	3	4	5
11. Illness of family member or self	1	2	3	4	5
12. Having to deal with stepfamily members	1	2	3	4	5
13. Having to move	1	2	3	4	5
14. Other _____	1	2	3	4	5
15. Other _____	1	2	3	4	5

Friendship Stressors

	1	2	3	4	5
1. Losing a friend	1	2	3	4	5
2. Not having enough friends	1	2	3	4	5
3. Having a friend reject me	1	2	3	4	5
4. Having a friend lie to me	1	2	3	4	5
5. Having a friend talk about me behind my back	1	2	3	4	5
6. Feeling unaccepted or disliked	1	2	3	4	5
7. Feeling left out	1	2	3	4	5
8. Having a friend my parents dislike or disapprove of	1	2	3	4	5
9. Worrying about not having a boyfriend or girlfriend	1	2	3	4	5
10. Not knowing how to make friends	1	2	3	4	5
11. Not knowing how to deal with situations involving friends	1	2	3	4	5
12. Not knowing how to stand up for my rights	1	2	3	4	5
13. Feeling unattractive	1	2	3	4	5
14. Other _____	1	2	3	4	5
15. Other _____	1	2	3	4	5

Teen Alert Questionnaire (TAQ)

Chapter Link

This questionnaire is to be used in conjunction with the Drugs and Alcohol chapter of *Helping the Struggling Adolescent*.

Rapid Assessment Description

This questionnaire is designed to give young people a quick picture of the seriousness of alcohol and drug problems.

Scoring Procedure

Young people who answer *Yes* to two of the TAQ questions may be at high risk for the development of the disease of chemical dependence. If they answer *Yes* to three of these questions, they have a problem with substance abuse. If they find it difficult to stop using mood-altering drugs for ninety days, they may already be chemically dependent. If they answer *Yes* to four or more of these questions, they already have many of the critical symptoms of chemical dependence. They need professional help as soon as possible.

Permission

Reprinted with permission of G. Douglas Talbott, M.D., clinical professor of psychiatry, Emory University.

Available from G. Douglas Talbott, M.D., Georgia Alcohol and Drug Associates, P.C., 1669 Phoenix Parkway, Suite 102, Atlanta, GA 30349.

TAQ

Please answer yes or no to the following questions. There are no right or wrong answers.

Yes   No   1. Have you ever felt the need to cut down on your alcohol or drug use?

Yes   No   2. Have you ever had a complete loss of memory (said or done things that you cannot remember) while under the influence of alcohol or drugs?

Yes   No   3. Do close relatives or friends ever worry or complain about your alcohol or drug use?

Yes   No   4. Have you ever been unable to stop drinking or using drugs when you wanted to?

Yes   No   5. Has your alcohol or drug use ever created problems between you and your parents, siblings, or friends?

Yes   No   6. Do you ever drink or use drugs in the morning?

Yes   No   7. Have you ever been told by a doctor, teacher, minister, or judge to stop drinking or using drugs?

Yes   No   8. Have you ever been arrested, even for a few hours, because of behavior while intoxicated or on drugs?

Yes   No   9. Do you have unexplained periods of depression, nervousness, anxiety, or difficulty with sleep?

Yes   No   10. Have you used either alcohol or drugs in the last week?

Yes   No   11. Have you been evasive or have you lied about the amount of drugs or alcohol you use?

Yes   No   12. Does your mother, father, brother, sister, or anyone else in your close family have a problem with alcohol or drugs?

Yes   No   13. Have you ever taken alcohol or drugs to school or used alcohol or drugs at school?

Yes   No   14. Have you ever made a promise to yourself or others that you would not drink or use drugs?

Yes   No   15. Is alcohol or drug use making it difficult for you to do your best at school, sports, hobbies, a job, or extracurricular activities?

Yes   No   16. Do you hide your alcohol, joints, or pills so that you will have a supply when your source is not available?

Yes   No   17. Have you ever skipped school or left school to use alcohol or drugs with friends or alone?

Yes   No   18. Have you ever been arrested, even for a few hours, because of driving while intoxicated on alcohol and/or on drugs?

Yes   No   19. Are you spending more time alone because of your alcohol or drugs?

Yes   No   20. Has alcohol or drugs affected your sexual activity or desire?

Yes   No   21. Have you noticed that you sometimes think of using alcohol or drugs at inappropriate times (that is, daydream or obsess about using)?

Yes   No   22. When people talk to you about your alcohol or drug use, do you feel angry, guilty, or uncomfortable?

Yes   No   23. Have you ever neglected your obligations and responsibilities to school, work, friends, or family because of drinking or drugs?

Yes   No   24. Have you ever been in the hospital, an emergency room, or sent to a doctor for an alcohol or drug problem?

Yes   No   25. Have you ever used alcohol or drugs when you were alone?

Tough Turf Peer Pressure Quiz (TTQ)

Chapter Link

This quiz is to be used in conjunction with the Peer Pressure chapter of *Helping the Struggling Adolescent.*

Rapid Assessment Description

This scale is an indicator of the degree to which peer pressure may influence a young person. Its items are derived from some of the most common types of pressure faced by young people.

Scoring Procedure

Add up the total of *Yes* responses. A score of 25 or more indicates the young person is more deeply affected by peer pressure. A score between 10 and 25 indicates peer pressure may affect the young person but not very much. A score between 0 and 10 indicates the young person probably has a great deal of self-confidence (if he or she is answering the questions honestly).

Permission

From *Tough Turf* by Bill Sanders (Old Tappan, N.J.: Revell, 1985; repr. Baker Book House). Reprinted by permission.

Available from Baker Book House, 6030 East Fulton Street, Ada, MI 49301.

TTQ

Please answer yes or no to the following questions. There are no right or wrong answers. Simply identify where you are now so you can see clearly where you want to go in the future.

Yes No   1. Do you wear the clothes you wear because you think others will approve?

Yes No   2. Do you keep from wearing clothing that you know is different from the trends or something that will surely get others' attention?

Yes No   3. Is your hairstyle "in"?

Yes No   4. If your hairstylist wanted to experiment on you, would you say no?

Yes No   5. If it were Fifties Day at your school, would you be too embarrassed to slick your hair back or wear a ponytail and white socks?

Yes No   6. Have you ever held back from trying to get top grades because the people you hang around with would not be comfortable?

Yes No   7. Have you ever joined in with others as they were "putting down" or laughing at another student?

Yes No   8. Would it be difficult for you to stop a fight or tell others not to pick on a certain student?

Yes No   9. Even if you wear your seatbelt when you ride in a car, do you ever hold back from asking others to wear theirs?

Yes No   10. Do you keep from wearing your seatbelt when someone else drives?

Yes No   11. Do you feel a strong need to go to college or get into a certain profession because "significant others" expect you to?

Yes No   12. Is it hard for you to approach your parents and discuss how you disagree with their expectations of you?

Yes No   13. Do you avoid showing affection to a family member while you are around other students?

Yes No   14. Do you avoid saying "I love you" to a family member or a close friend?

Yes No   15. If you wore braces, would it be hard for you to smile?

Yes No   16. Do you feel embarrassed if others snicker at one of your questions in class?

Yes No   17. Is it hard for you to ask disruptive students to be quiet during class?

Yes No   18. Do you go to parties at which you feel uncomfortable?

Yes No   19. At parties do you ever do things you don't believe in?

Yes   No   20. Do you watch or listen to TV programs, movies, and "in" music even though you don't agree with them?

Yes   No   21. Would it be hard for you to walk out of a movie if you were offended, even if you were with a group of friends?

Yes   No   22. Do you avoid sitting in a different place with different students in the cafeteria?

Yes   No   23. Have you ever wanted to go out for a sport or the school play but did not?

Yes   No   24. Do you steal things or cheat on tests because a friend does?

Yes   No   25. Do you lie because your friends expect you to?

Yes   No   26. Is it hard for you to go to your parents with your problems and concerns?

Yes   No   27. Have you ever had a great idea but felt ashamed to tell anyone or share it in class?

Yes   No   28. Do you often disagree with your teacher but never say anything?

Yes   No   29. Have you ever felt like complimenting your teacher but didn't?

Yes   No   30. Is it hard for you to arrive early and stay later and work harder than other employees where you work?

Yes   No   31. Do you avoid praying before meals when you are out with friends?

Yes   No   32. Are you ashamed to share your religious convictions with other people, even if they ask?

Yes   No   33. Would it be hard for you to stay after practice (for any sport) and work out, even if others scoffed at you?

Yes   No   34. Is it difficult for you to tell a friend, "I am going to stay home tonight and work on my term paper"?

Yes   No   35. If you knew someone was ruining his life with drugs, would it be a tough decision for you to get him the help he needs?

Yes   No   36. Would it be tough for you to go to a party and drink a Dr. Pepper if you knew everyone else was drinking booze and would make fun of you?

Yes   No   37. If several students were leaving a party totally "blitzed," would it be embarrassing for you to persuade them not to drive, but to ride with you?

Yes   No   38. If a fellow student had a real emptiness in her heart and she felt she had nothing to live for, would you find it difficult to tell her about God or get her in touch with a counselor?

Yes   No   39. If you saw your boss stealing from the company you work for, would you confront him or her?

Yes   No   40. Is it almost impossible for you to invite a younger brother or sister to do something with you where you will be seen by your peers?

Les Parrott III, Ph.D., is associate professor of clinical psychology and director of the Center for Relationship Development at Seattle Pacific University. Dr. Parrott is also a Fellow in Medical Psychology at the University of Washington School of Medicine. He is an ordained minister and the author of numerous articles and books. He received the doctorate from the Fuller Graduate School of Psychology.